Dr. Angela Gordon-Nichols, Ed.D.

MOTIVATION

Inside The Mind of the African American Collegiate Football Player

This body of research is a work of non-fiction. It was compiled of the author's personal efforts in conjunction with researchers who have been cited within.

CLF Publishing, LLC.
www.clfpublishing.org
909.315.3161

Copyright © 2012 by Angela Gordon-Nichols. All rights reserved. No portion of this book may be reproduced, stored in a retrieval system, or transmitted by any form or any means electronically, photocopied, recorded, or any other except for brief quotations in printed reviews, without the prior permission of the publisher.

Cover design by Senir Design. Contact information: info@senirdesign.com.

ISBN # 978-1-945102-51-6

Printed in the United States of America.

DEDICATION

I dedicate this research to my husband of 38 years, Arnold Nichols. The Yang to my Yin. Thank you for tolerating the long nights of report writing and participating in many of my experiments. You are an "awesome husband," you earned this degree with me.

I dedicate this research to my children, Chanel, Porsche, and Arnold II, you are my jewels. You fill my treasure box with the brightness of your hearts. Thank you for the many contributions you made. Stay on your paths. I'm waiting for you to meet me here.

This is dedicated to all of my sisters, Dorothy, Gloria, and Carolyn. To my extended family members, and friends whose love and support have helped turn this once lifelong dream into a shared reality. Thank you.

To those who motivated me the most, you know who you are, thanks for giving me a reason to keep moving forward. I'm still smiling.

Last but not least, I dedicate this to my mother, Dorothy Gordon. Thank you for providing me with the foundation of psychology as I grew up. My degree is because of you. One day "Jack Ego" will get his recognition. I love you, mom.

To God Be The Glory!
"For the Lord is good; his mercy is everlasting; and his truth endureth to all generations."
Psalm 100:5

ACKNOWLEDGEMENTS

First giving honor to God, who is the source of my strength. He is the true author and finisher of my life and the director of my path.

This author would like to express sincere gratitude to my committee members, Dr. Akin Merino, Ph.D., Dr. Debra Murphy, Psy. D., and Dr. Michael McCormick, Psy. D. Their invaluable support and guidance in the planning and implementation of this research project will not be forgotten.

Much love and appreciation to the many male African American student-athletes and coaches who did not fall in the range of this study, but were willing to make themselves transparent, wanting to contribute words of wisdom to this research idea. Thank you.

Last but not least, my heart and prayers are with the three young men who made themselves most transparent and vulnerable to make this research project possible. Without their gift of time and thoughts, this study would not have been achievable. Success for them is on the way. I know they will stay focused, diligent, and faithful. One day their star will shine bright.

TABLE OF CONTENTS

CHAPTER ONE: THE PROBLEM 9
Time Management 12
Phase 1 – History of College Football 13
    Diversity in College Football 13
Phase II – Self Actualization – Athletic Program vs. Academic Program Counseling 16
Phase III – Career Planning – Where Are They Going? 19
Purpose 20
Significance of Study 20
Research Questions 20
Definitions of Terms 20
Overview of Study 22

CHAPTER TWO: REVIEW OF THE LITERATURE 23
What are the learning styles of the African American male athlete?
    Learning Style Model 24
    Personality Preferences 26
How do African American Male Student-Athletes Develop Their Learning Styles? 28
How Do the African American Student-Athletes Apply Their Learning Styles to Motivation and Their Perception of Being Successful in College? 32
    Reading and Motivation 36
The Interest Convergence Principle 40
National Collegiate Athletic Association (NCAA) and Male Student-Athletes 42

CHAPTER THREE: METHODOLOGY 44
Data Collection and Fieldwork Strategies 46
Population and Sampling 47
    Population Sampling 47

    Non-Probability Sampling 47

    Sampling Used for This Research 48

    Participant Eligibility 48

    Research Question Guideline 50

Data Collection 50

Data Analysis 52

Limitations 53

Delimitations 53

CHAPTER FOUR: FINDINGS 54

Purpose 55

Contents 55

Demographics 55

Data Management 55

    Participant Profiles 56

    Interview Narrative and Themes 57

        Question 1 58

        Question 2 58

        Question 3 59

        Question 4 59

        Question 5 60

        Question 6 60

        Question 7 61

        Question 8 62

        Question 9 62

        Question 10 63

        Question 11 63

        Question 12 64

Data Analysis 66

Summary of Findings.. 67
    Explanation of Themes 67
    Additional Results..76
        Abraham...76
        Martin 76
        John..77

CHAPTER FIVE: DISCUSSION...80
Summary of Investigation..80
    What are the learning styles of the male African American college football athlete?...81
    Is there a learning style that predominates for the male African American Football Student-Athlete?..82
        Howard Gardener's Eight Ways of Learning…..………………………..83
    Does the male African American college football student-athlete apply his learning styles to motivate his career decision-making perception?...............86
        Learning Disabilities 88
Emerging Themes 89
Erickson Psychosocial Theory 89
Additional Findings 91
Contributions of Findings 92
Andragogy Learning 94
Theory Implications 96
Practice Implications..96
Limitations 97
Recommendations for Future Research 97
Summary 98

REFERENCES...100

TABLE OF FIGURES

1. Three Phases That Could Influence Learning Styles 11
2. Self-Actualization of the Student Athlete 75
3. Identity vs. Role Confusion of the Student Athlete 90
4. Andragogy Transformation..92

TABLE OF APPENDICES

A. Transcriptions of Interviews 110
B. Initial List of Themes 151
C. Cluster of Themes 157
D. Table of Themes..162
E. Framework for Identifying Themes and Thinking Process.......................................171
F. Emerging Theme Chart..174

The David A. Kolb styles model is based on the Experiential Learning Theory (ELT), as explained in his book *Experiential Learning: Experience as the Source of Learning and Development* (1984). The ELT model outlines two related approaches toward grasping experience: Concrete Experience (must be involved in new experiences) and Abstract Conceptualization (create theories to explain experience). It also outlines two related approaches toward transforming experience: Reflective Observation (watches others or observes self to explain action) and Active Experimentation (uses theories to solve problems). According to Kolb's model, the ideal learning process engages all four of these modes in response to situational demands. In order for learning to be effective, all four of these approaches must be incorporated. As individuals attempt to use all four approaches, however, they tend to develop strengths in one experience-grasping approach and one experience-transforming approach. The resulting learning styles are combinations of the individual's preferred approaches.

The learning styles for Kolb (1984) include four styles, Diverging/Reflectors, Assimilating/Theorists, Converging/Pragmatists and Accommodating/Activists. These styles of learning include persons who need to think about the activity/concept as well as observe it to those who would prefer jumping into the activity/concept and trying it out. Kolb (1984) states that all these learning styles may happen in a flash, or over days, weeks or months, depending on the topic, and there may be a "wheels within wheels" process at the same time.

According the Dr. Jawanza Kunjufu (2010), knowing how African American males learn is the secret to teaching them. According to Dr. Kunjufu, teaching the male African American according to his learning style preference will enhance his success rate in higher education. This research will seek to study not only how the African American male learns how to learn, but in particular the African American college football student-athlete learning styles.

To better understand the current influence of college football and its relationship to male African American recruitment, this research will initially examine historical influences in football history. Presenting the history of college football and how it influenced the male African American so profoundly, will provide information that will lend to a better understanding of how the male African American college student-athlete learns.

After examining the history of college football and its relationship to the male African American student-athlete, this research will look at the current learning styles of the African American males who attend college as student-athletes.

Three phases of learning style influences may contribute to an athlete's learning style development and his ability to be successful in his sport and education. (see Figure 1).

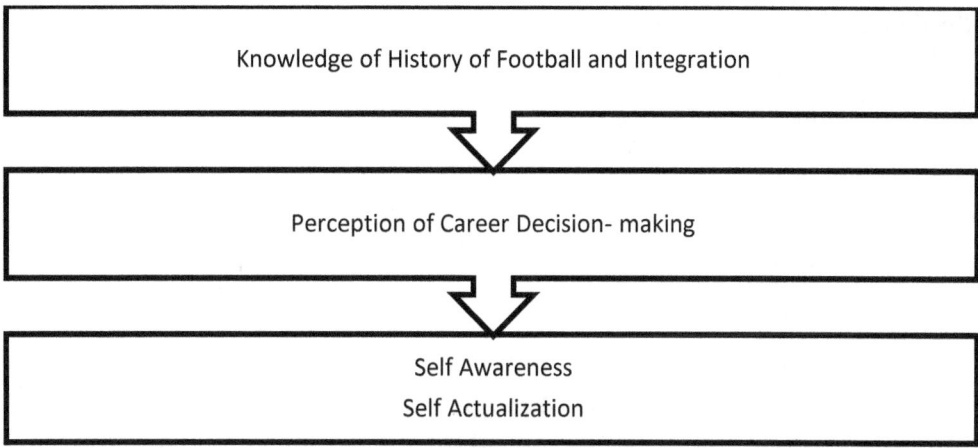

Figure 1. The three phases of learning style influences which can affect the learning style development of the student-athlete.

The first phase would be learning the history of the sport and its influence on the student-athlete perception of being given the opportunity to play integrated college football and to pursue education. According to Ferguson (2009), when looking at the history of the African American college football student-athlete, it is the social dilemmas within and outside of the African American male's community that can distort what options appear to be obtainable for their futures.

The second phase for the developing African American male college student-athlete would be for him to learn self-awareness and self-actualization of where he is in his sport and academics as he prepares to be a college athlete. Ferguson (2009) defined this phase as part of stage four in Erickson's eight stages of psychosocial development, Industry vs. Inferiority. She also reported that when the African American student-athlete revisits Industry vs. Inferiority, he will interpret productiveness via recognition from others in the form of being respected, challenged, supported, and held accountable for his actions. By achieving stability and accomplishing certain tasks, the African American student-athlete's perception of his opportunity to develop confidence in both his intellectual and athletic abilities develops (Ferguson, 2009).

Identity versus role confusion may also play a part in phase three. According to Erickson (1950, p. 261), people become "concerned with what they appear to be in the eyes of others as compared with what they feel they are." Ferguson (2009) stated that the African American college student-athlete becomes very concerned about how he is perceived by others; as the student-athlete revisits this stage he may over-identify with a particular identity or demonstrate a loss of identity. All of which may affect his learning style preference.

The third phase is for the athlete's perception of what he wants his career path to look like and how he develops a plan for being successful on that path as well as developing the insight to develop an alternative plan should something go wrong. These decisions would be reflective of phases one and two and how he learned how to learn while going through them. The third phase would also include the athlete's ability to manage time, a critical element the challenge to balance being an athlete and a student (See figure 1.1).

Time Management

According to Cornell University, Division of Nutritional Science (2011), the biggest challenges to the student-athlete are time issues. These issues arise at the level of daily planning, semester-long planning and even planning their four years. The university reports that athletes have to use the same discipline they use in their sports to ensure that they use the time available to them between classes and before and after practice and competitions to complete their assignments and prepare for exams. The Division of Nutritional Science at Cornell University (2011) reports that one of the biggest changes from high school that many athletes experience in college is the expectation that they will be actively involved in the planning of their course of study and their future careers. Many student-athletes are not prepared for the changes that present themselves in college. In particular, the university states that a student-athlete must learn what his special academic strengths are, as well as those areas that are weak and need to be strengthened. The student-athlete must learn how to use his strengths and improve his weaknesses. Time management is a critical part of the strength and weakness assessment for a student-athlete. As a part of the three phases of a developing male African American student-athlete, time management is one a student-athlete should develop in order to balance athletic commitments with academic commitments during the career decision-making phase.

This research seeks to inquire what the male African American college football student-athletes' learning styles are. Three phases have been prementioned as possible influences to the learning style. This research will aim to examine whether the male African American college football student-athlete's learning styles are influenced by them.

Phase I - History of College Football

According to John Cassara (2011), the birth of college football occurred on November 6, 1869. In 1869, teams from the Princeton and Rutgers Universities met in New Brunswick, New York, for the first intercollegiate football game. Cassara (2011) reported that at the end of World War II, college football student-athletes began to receive athletic scholarships, which increased in numbers quickly. It reports that today nearly every major college football student-athlete is paid room, board, tuition, and other expenses, with funds derived usually from donations from alumni and game profits. Scholarships are used as incentives to encourage football student-athletes as a whole to develop skills in the sport (Cassara, 2011). Scholarships are especially attractive to the low income African American male. Nearly all major college football teams are members of either the National Collegiate Athletic Association (NCAA) or the National Association of Inter-collegiate Athletics (NAIA), which implement the rules and oversee competition between teams. Most of the major universities are grouped in conferences, such as the Big Ten, the Pacific Ten, the Big Eight, the Southeastern Conference, the Southwestern Athletic Conference and the Ivy League (Banks, 2005). College teams usually play eleven games a season.

Saylor (2011) reported that the Historical African American Colleges and Universities (HBCU) began to develop football programs to compensate for not being able to play at the predominantly White colleges in 1892. He reports that during the years 1930 to 2004, football in the historically African American colleges can be divisible into three eras, the dividing points being World War II, the Civil Rights Act of 1964, and the current football status of the Historical African American Colleges and Universities (HBCU).

Diversity in College Football

According to John Cassara (2011), the initial sport of football was not designed to include male African Americans (Cassara, 2011). It was only after the 1970s that African American participation in the college sport grew larger. The last colleges to desegregate were in the Southeastern Conference in the early 1970s. Male African American student-athletes were first accepted in the northern states. Unfortunately, northern integrated football teams were frequently unaccepted on the college football fields of southern colleges (Cassara, 2011). From the 19th Century to the 1970s (80 years), hostility toward African American participation in the sport was prevalent throughout much of the country. John Cassara (2011) stated that in the years 1890 to 1919, hostility took the form of what came to be known as the "Gentlemen's Agreement" (Cassara, 2011). The Gentlemen's Agreement was an unwritten agreement between colleges that would bind

Northern colleges not to use colored student-athletes when teams from the South played in the North. In spite of the obstacles male African American college football student-athletes encountered, and the racism they had to face, almost all of these African American college student-athlete pioneers enjoyed tremendous success both on and off the field. "They learned to accept their difficulties with an opportunity to excel both athletically and academically" (Cassara, 2011, p. 1).

As college football integration transitioned after World War I and through World War II, a period lasting from 1920 to 1945, the number of male African American college football student-athletes at predominantly white universities in the north began growing significantly, and many of these student-athletes became stars. Despite their increasing numbers in the sport, male African Americans who played during this period continued to be confronted with being subjected to the "Gentleman's Agreement" (Cassara, 2011) of the south.

In the late 1930s and early 1940s, more male African American student-athletes had the opportunity to play in games against segregated southern schools (Cassara, 2011). At the end of this period, cases where the "Gentleman's Agreement" was actually invoked would often be protested by students and media (particularly the African American press), who were cognizant of what was taking place at the game. Examples of African American student-athletes being allowed to play in intersectional contests and of large-scale protests against the "Gentleman's Agreement" in the Southern states was an indication of what was to come in the ensuing years (Cassara, 2011).

According to Roger Saylor (2011), by 1930 the HBCU answered the challenges developed by the gentleman's agreement by fielding teams in all the states which had been part of the Confederacy during the Civil War plus the border states of Delaware, Kentucky, Maryland, and Missouri, and the portion of Virginia which became West Virginia. Oklahoma, not yet then a state, had established Langston as its college for African Americans and was represented.

By the end of World War II, 1946 -1956, there were great changes occurring in America, particularly in race-relations (Cassara, 2011). The country was realizing that it "could not claim to be the most democratic nation in the world and still make allowances for institutionalized segregation and discrimination throughout much of its land." It was the Brown v. Board of Education Supreme Court decision in 1954 which had the greatest impact (Cassara, 2011). This court decision determined that separate education in public schools for African American and White was unconstitutional. According to college football historian John Sayle Watterson (2000), the end of the World War II also marked a clear "turning point" for college football, as the changing racial attitudes across the country had their effect on the college football fields (p. 312). He reported that the racial make-up of college football rosters outside the south became increasingly

African American, and college football officials outside the south almost universally "refused to concede to southern racial demands" (p. 312). The gentleman's agreement was slowly becoming obsolete, as southern schools were being forced to take the field against integrated teams more often.

According to Roger Saylor (2011), most of the early best HBCU football programs that were powerful on the football field of play continued in that role through World War II. During the 1950s, southern schools found themselves no longer able to dictate college football's racial politics. As historian Kurt Kemper (2004) wrote, Southern teams found fewer and fewer schools willing to schedule games under a Gentlemen's Agreement. Southern schools adjusted to this by playing integrated teams on the road, thereby not offending fans or state laws at home, but still enabling them to play the key intersectional games for which Southern fans so longed. Eventually, integrated schools intensified their refusal to play Southern schools at all (Cassara, 2011).

The civil rights movement had the biggest effect on the desegregation of the college football. The movement of the 1960s confirmed that reform was inevitable, and Southern schools found themselves being affected by the shift to desegregate their rosters if for no other reason than to remain relevant and competitive in the national college football scene. In the fall of 1961, students at the University of California, Los Angeles threatened to boycott the Rose Bowl if it meant playing a segregated University of Alabama team. By 1972 the University of Mississippi became the last school in the Southeastern Conference to desegregate its team. It was their game against the University of Southern California (USC) that ended institutionalized segregation in college football. The game served as a conclusion to the 80 plus year process of integration in the game (Cassara, 2011).

On January 7, 2009, HBO Sports released a documentary entitled *"Breaking the Huddle, The Integration of College Football"* which highlighted the many challenges of the early male African American college football student-athletes. These were student-athletes who reaped the benefits of the 1970s, as they changed. Some of those interviewed were Darryl Hill, who spoke about how Martin Luther King's speech, "I Have a Dream," helped him navigate through the racism being experienced on and off the field, and about how he played on football fields where his mother was unable to sit in the stands and watch the games. Another student-athlete from the civil rights era interviewed was Wilber Hackett, Jr. who played for the University of Kentucky. He talked about the evolution of football and how African Americans have more opportunities available to play for Predominantly White Institutions (PWIs) than ever before (Rhoden, 2008).

The Central Broadcasting Services (CBS) showed a documentary on the *"The Football Game that Broke Racial Barriers"* on October 25, 2006. The documentary was based on the 1970

University of Southern California (USC) versus University of Alabama (U of A) game. According to CBS, this game was used to demonstrate to white fans of the University of Alabama that football could be a better played game if African American student-athletes were included in what was at that time an all-White football team. The team was in need of bigger and stronger student-athletes on their team to increase their winning capabilities and the head coach, Paul Bryant, believed in order to have a strong playing football team, it needed to have African American student-athletes on it. Paul Bryant met with head coach of USC, John Mc Kay, to play an exhibition football game against each other. USC was already a fully integrated football team. USC won the game 42-21. Eddie Pells (2010), of Diverse Issues in Education writes:

> The boilerplate story is that Bryant wanted that game against USC to show to the Crimson Tide faithful the kind of football a roster filled with great athletes, African American and White, could really produce.
>
> USC ran for 485 yards and won 42-21. Regardless of whether Bryant specifically acknowledged after the game that Alabama could use African American student-athletes— as the old story goes— the point had been proven: To win at the highest level, teams needed the best student-athletes, and picking from a Whites-only talent pool was no longer a realistic option.
>
> "The reality was that guys wanted to win," said John David Briley, author of *Career in Crisis: Paul 'Bear' Bryant* and *The 1971 Season of Change*. "It didn't matter what color the student-athletes were, they wanted to win."

Football recruitment does not necessarily take into consideration the effect of the possibly inferior education the student-athlete may have received during K thru 12th grade and how his education may have a negative effect on his learning style and perception of his future. According to Ferguson (2010), the process of being recruited is the period that institutions deliver messages about the importance or lack of importance of academics. She states that the recruiting visit is a pivotal moment for the African American student-athlete who may lack academic support. The visit can serve as a form of coercion or inducement because the recruit "unwisely may choose an institution in which he will not realize adequate progress toward his educational or career goals" because of his fixation on athletic opportunity.

Phase II – Self-Actualization - Athletic Programs vs. Academic Program Counseling

Phase II is when the student-athlete begins to develop his self-esteem and self-actualization. Using Maslow's Theory of Motivation (1954), this phase is when the student-athlete comes to the full realization of his potential. The male African American athlete's need to succeed will develop into his hierarchy of necessities which may be influenced by his environmental, cultural, economic, ethnic, and social needs. This research will seek to explore the possibility of the male African American student-athlete developing a need to excel in academics concurrently with the need to excel in his sport during this phase.

While college student-athletic programs are improving, according to Banks (2005), many athletic programs in the past have lacked professional counselors or mental health workers on their staff. It is the lack of professional counselors or mental health workers missing from most athletic program staff that may have serve as a contributor to what would appear to be the mis-education of the African American student college football athlete, according to Banks (2005). Most colleges have had student athletic advisors who are neither trained in counseling or any psychology-related disciplines (Banks, 2005). Consequently, most programs have academic advisors for basic class schedules, tutoring, and time management advice (Banks, 2005).

These advisors were not cognizant of the learning style and development of the African American college football athlete when issuing out advice to them (Banks, 2005). Self-actualization may not be assessed in the student unless there is an obvious deficit in his ability to be successful in his sport (Banks, 2005). Many colleges have recently discovered this oversight in athletic academia and are now making efforts to change their programs (Banks, 2005). Many are realizing the importance of the academic needs, personal and athletic issues of the new student-athlete (Banks, 2005). This realization is primarily the result of the National Collegiate Athletic Association (NCAA) developing new guidelines for colleges who are not graduating a sufficient amount of student-athletes (Hosick, 2011). The NCAA has now started issuing penalties to colleges for not preparing student-athletes for life after football. There have been gaps in research in the area of student-athlete learning styles and now that more recognition has been focused on the gap, research is increasing in the twenty-first century, evident by the availability of more current information for this research.

According to Banks (2005), there have been few studies that use developmental models when studying the African American college football student-athlete. Additionally, Banks (2005) reported that there has been minimal attention given to providing counseling services to student-athletes over the years since football integration that have addressed the developmental needs of this group.

Banks (2005) also noted that there is widely reported contention that the social and intellectual development of African American college students is nurtured better by Traditionally African American Collegiate Institutions (TBIs) than by Predominantly White Collegiate

Institutions (PWIs). It was hypothesized that if the reported environmental effects exist, then students at TBIs ought to be more developmentally advanced than their counterparts at PWIs. However, the results of their study did not provide clear support for the superiority of the TBIs in facilitating the development of African American college students.

In 1994, Timothy Wilson and Barbara Banks revealed their perspective on the education of the African American child, especially the male. They stated that the education of African American children requires special consideration. In the past, they have been disproportionally labeled as mentally retarded and placed in special classes. In the 21st century, misplacing male African Americans in special classes, continue to be a problem. They have also received disproportionate corporal punishments as compared to their European-American counterparts. Wilson and Banks (1994) have proposed that the old beliefs and values system must be replaced with new productive ideas and strategies in order to effectively educate the male African American.

While this study focuses on the male African American college student-athlete, in order to understand his learning styles, some research into how the student-athlete learns in high school and middle school is necessary. In the *Journal of Negro Education*, an article written by Serie McDougal (2009) entitled, *"Break It Down," One of the Cultural and Stylist Instructional Preferences of African American Males"* was found. McDougal conducted one-on-one interviews with 29 students. The selection of interviewees was carried out with the assistance of a web-based random selection program. Identification numbers were assigned to each potential student interviewee and a list of student identification numbers was generated in random sequence. This list was used to determine which potential subjects were chosen to be interviewed, and the sequence in which those interviews would take place. Interviews with students were conducted to assess how they perceive how they learn the best, and the strategies they use to make sure that they reach the fullest understanding of academic information.

McDougal (2009) reported that 45% of the students interviewed expressed they have a preference for, and they benefit from being provided a certain type of explanation from their teachers. Students expressed their desire to know if what they were learning will be important for them in their everyday lives or "the real world" (McDougal, 2009). Students explained that they learn best when a teacher not only gave them an assignment or directions for an assignment, but when a teacher *broke it down* or explained how to do a given assignment or how to engage in a given process step by step, in easily understandable language (McDougal, 2009). This was the most common stylistic preference students expressed in interviews with regard to how information is presented to them. Other preferences students mentioned in interviews were the use of visual aids and tactile or kinesthetic hands-on learning.

This learning style is consistent with Gardener's Nine Intelligences (1999) and in particular, the direction of this research that the learning styles for the male African American college football student-athlete are more kinesthetic action related.

Phase III – Career Planning – Where Are They Going?

Past educational systems have failed the African American male because they have concentrated on molding them to fit into a system that was not developed for them (Wilson and Banks, 1994). As a result the system has not worked and is failing the average African American male (Kunjufu, 2010). Kunjufu (2010) noted the importance of the educational system becoming more effective for the African American male. He states that a universal plan has not been developed that is conducive to the African American learning styles and that the lack of a universal educational system addressing the learning styles of the male African American student-athlete has affected the college graduation success rate.

According to New America Media, Eboni Farmer (2009), *Colleges Fight to Get and Keep African American Males,* programs across the country are now implementing mentorship programs to keep African American males in college. The programs are designed to support initiatives such as the African American Male Initiative in the Georgia State System, which is focused on reducing the gap between the enrollment, retention, and graduation rates of African American males and females.

Per Eboni Farmer (2009), athletes are more successful in college if there is an African American Student Union or another culturally supported program on the college campus. These programs recognize the need to "reinstall" guidance that the student received in junior high school and high school (p. 1). This would also include tapping into the learning styles of the male African American. Ironically, Farmer also noted that Historically Black African American Colleges and Universities (HBCU) have a lower graduation rate (22%) than predominately White colleges (96–98 %). The thematic reason for low graduation rates continues to be that most of the African American males come from lower income households, not prepared for collegiate academics, lacking the skills they should have gotten at home and in the classroom. Farmer reported that this is a consistent conclusion with African American men at colleges and universities across the board whether it is a predominantly White school or an HBCU.

This research will examine whether a male African American college football student-athlete learns to identify his learning style and work within it. It will seek to examine the male African American football student-athlete's learning style, learning style development, and his learning style/decision-making.

Purpose

The purpose of this study is to explore the learning styles of the male African American college football athlete. It will seek to discover how the male African American college football athlete learns how to learn and how he uses his learning style in his career decision-making perception.

Significance of Study

The data collected from this research will lend to the contribution of knowledge and theories relative to this phenomenon and be a guide for evaluating existing programs and policies.

Research Questions

1. What are the learning styles of the male African American college football athlete?
2. Is there a learning style that predominates for the male African American football student-athlete?
3. Does the male African American college football student-athlete apply his learning styles to motivate his career decision-making perception?

Definition of Terms

Academic Identity. The challenges in the educational development which includes serious stifling of achievement, aspiration, and pride in school systems.

Achievement Motivation. Determines our successes and aspirational achievements in life.

Afrocentric Paradigm. The culture experiences and perceptions of people of African descent must be at the center of any human enterprise dealing with people of African descent.

Andragogy. The focus of teaching shifts from the teacher to the learner, the adult. The learner is in control over what is learned.

Athletic Identity. The degree to which an individual identifies with the athlete role.

Barriers to Identity. Educational tracking that locks African American males into substandard classes and ineffective classroom learning environments.

Career Maturity. The individual's ability to make appropriate career choices, including what is required to make a career decision and the degree to which one's choices are both realistic and consistent over time.

Ethnic Identity. Ethnic identity is the extent to which one identifies with a particular ethnic group(s). It refers to one's sense of belonging to an ethnic group and the part of one's thinking, perceptions, feelings, and behavior that is due to ethnic group membership. The ethnic group tends to be one in which the individual claims heritage (Phinney, 1996). Ethnic identity is separate from one's personal identity as an individual, although the two may reciprocally influence each other.

External Motivation. Sources outside of oneself that motivates a person.

Internal Motivation. The need to accomplish goals comes from within oneself.

Identity Foreclosure. The state of mind an individual has while he is committed to an occupation or ideology without considering or exploring additional options.

Interest Convergence. Defined as an act of interest in African Americans achieving racial equality based on the accommodation being provided only when it converges with the interests of Whites.

Maslow's Hierarchy of Needs, also referred to as the Theory of Motivation. Represented in a hierarchical pyramid with five levels. The four levels (lower-order needs – physiological, safety, belongingness, and esteem) are considered *physiological needs,* while the top level (self-actualization) is considered a *growth need.*

Mental Self-Management. Also known as metacognition and is the art of planning, monitoring, and evaluating the learning process.

Multiple Intelligences. Cognitive functions the talents are the behaviors that indicate performance in intelligent activity. It is the manifest endpoint and product of a process that is behavioral and dependent on specific pre-existing cognate functions.

Pedagogy. This usually refers to the teaching of children, where the teacher is the focal point and in control of what is taught.

Psychosocial Development. The eight stages of development introduced by Erik Erickson through which a healthily developing human should pass from infancy to late adulthood.

Social Identity. This theory indicates that group membership creates in-group/self-categorization and enhancement in ways that favor the in-group at the expense of the out-group.

Social Cognitive Career Theory. Focuses on the connection of self-efficacy, outcome expectations and personal goals that influence an individual's career choice.

Overview of the Study

Chapter 1 consists of the researcher's statement of the problem, the purpose of the research, the significance of the study, the research questions, and the definition of terms used for this research. Chapter 2 examines literary research on the learning styles of the African American male college football student-athlete, how the African American male college football student-athlete develops his learning styles, and how the African American male football student-athlete applies his learning styles to his career decision-making perception. Chapter 3 discusses the research method for this study. It will include the population and sampling, research style used, data collection, research analysis, limitations of the study, and the delimitations of the study. Chapter 4 includes information about the results of interviews conducted, commonalities among the group as well as findings that were not common. Chapter 5 includes recommendations for future studies and suggested systematic implementations that may affect the learning styles of the male African American male football student-athlete.

CHAPTER TWO: REVIEW OF THE LITERATURE

What Are the Learning Styles of the African American Male student-athlete?

In Chapter One, reference was made to a 1994 journal article by Timothy Wilson and Barbara Banks in which they revealed their perspective on the education of the African American child, especially the male. They expressed their belief that the school system is failing these students. In 2010, according to Dr. Jawanza Kunjufu, "Schools fail boys in many ways, not only are they resistant to change, many programs that are perfect for high-energy, right-brain learners, such as physical education and the arts, have been virtually eliminated in schools." Kunjufu (2010) is the author of the book *Understanding African American Male Learning Styles* and has developed a learning style model for the male African American. He stated that the secret to teaching them is to understand how they learn. He believes that if teachers teach to a student's learning styles, create stimulating, culturally relevant learning environments, African American boys will excel in school. According to Kunjufu (2010), "Even though girls mature academically at a faster pace than boys, boys are expected to read and master fine motor movements before they are ready. Boys are excellent at doing complicated NBA math, NFL math, rap math, and drug math, yet they are failing basic math and algebra in school." Kunjufu's Learning Styles Model is based on the biological propensity for learning introduced by Dr. Rita Dunn.

Rita Dunn and her husband Kenneth developed the Dunn & Dunn Learning Styles Model. In their book, *Teaching Students Through Their Individual Learning Styles: A Practical Approach*, they provide background on how learners are affected by elements of the classroom and follow it with recommendations of how to accommodate students' learning strengths. Dunn and Dunn write that "learners are affected by their: (a) immediate environment (sound, light, temperature, and design); (b) own emotionality (motivation, persistence, responsibility, and need for structure or flexibility); (c) sociological needs (self, pair, peers, team, adult, or varied); and (d) physical needs (perceptual strengths, intake, time, and mobility)." They analyzed other research and made the claim that not only can students identify their preferred learning styles, but students also score higher on tests, have better attitudes, and are more efficient if they are taught in ways to which they can more easily relate. Therefore, it is to the educator's advantage to teach and test students in their preferred styles.

The Learning Style Model

Kunjufu's Learning Style Model (2010) enhances Dunn and Dunn's theory by designing a model to help educators understand how the male African American student learns. He proposed three basic categories of learners:

1. Visual Learner
    a. Visual-Print
    b. Visual-Pictures
2. Oral/Auditory Learners
3. Tactile/Kinesthetic Learners

These three basic categories are representative of right-brain learners. Kunjufu stated that approximately two-thirds of students and an even larger percentage of African American males are visual-picture, oral/auditory, and tactile/kinesthetic learners. He observed that most of the learning activities conducted in schools are more focused on left-brain learners, who more frequently use the visual-print approach.

It appears that 17 years later, after Timothy Wilson and Barbara Banks discussed African American male education needing a new approach, teachers still have not adjusted pedagogy to meet their needs. According to Dr. Kunjufu (2010), the African American male is now in a state of academic emergency. Teachers have not learned to teach the way the African American children learn.

Madge Gill Willis (2002) introduced and reviewed Boykin's (1983) nine dimensions of learning styles of African American Children. She found them to be spirituality, harmony, movement, verve, affect, communalism, expressive individualism, orality, and social time perspective. From Boykin's (1983) dimensions, Willis (2002) found that the key factors for African American learning are cooperation and communication styles. When teachers teach according to the learning styles of the African American child, curriculum should be integrated into four groupings to promote successful teaching. They should be people-oriented because social interaction is crucial and social learning is common. In Willis's view, the teaching experience should be holistic and incorporate experiences and seek synthesis. The teacher must also address the learning style by encouraging adaptive, variable, intuitive, and novel creativity that will produce continual stimulation. Among the most important contributions to learning styles is what is perceived non-verbally. The non-verbal response of a teacher is also very affective on the learning style of the African American student. According to Willis, movement and rhythm components are vital to the learning style of the African American child.

Personality Preferences

Another perspective to look at when examining the male African American student-athlete football student-athlete is their personality preferences. Reiter, Liput, Nirmal, (2007) studied the personality preferences of college student-athletes. They found no major statistical differences between the athletes and the non-athletes. However, several of the results seemed noteworthy and are presented.

Reiter, Liput, and Nirmal's (2007) research was based on the notion that being involved with competitive sports, usually for many years, may have an impact on a person's personality, or perceived sense of personality, the purpose of this study was to determine whether there were differences in perceived personality preferences between college student-athletes and college non-athletes.

Participants were recruited through a convenience sampling technique from various areas of a large private southeastern university. The data consisted of 91 undergraduate students from a large NCAA Division II Southeastern university who volunteered to take the Myers-Briggs Type Indicator (MBTI), Reiter, Liput, and Nirmal's (2007). The Myers-Briggs Type Indicator (MBTI) assessment is a psychometric questionnaire designed to measure psychological preferences in how people perceive the world and make decisions.

Data analysis consisted of scoring the MBTI for each participant and comparing scores on each of the eight personality characteristic scales (E, I, S, N, T, F, J, P), t-tests were used to determine differences on each of the indices between the college student-athletes and the nonathletes, Reiter, Liput, and Nirmal's (2007). As shown in Table 1, eight personality characteristic scales for MBTI are referred to as dichotomies. The dichotomies are presented with personality preferences and psychological areas affected:

Table 1

Myers Briggs Type Indicator Table

Dichotomy	The Preference	Psychological Area
Extraversion	Prefers the outer world of people and things.	Attitudes
Introversion	More interested in the inner world of ideas.	Attitudes
Sensing	Focus on the present and on concrete information gained from their senses.	Perception
i**N**tuition	Focus on the future with a view toward patterns and possibilities. Prefer to receive data from the subconscious or seeing relationships via insights.	Perception
Thinking	Tend to base their decisions on logic "true or false, if-then" connections and on objective analysis of cause and effect. Decide with their head.	Decision making calculus functions.
Feeling	Tend to base their decisions on values and on subjective evaluation of person centered concerns. They use "more or less, better or worse" evaluations. Decide with their heart.	Decision making calculus functions.
Judging	Tend to like a planned and organized approach to life and prefer to have things settled.	Used to deal with the outside world.
Perceiving	Flexible and spontaneous approach to life and prefer to keep their options open.	Used to deal with the outside world.

Reiter, Liput, and Nirmal's (2007) found that 51% of the student-athletes scored in favor of sensing, whereas 62% of the non-athletes scored in favor of intuition. student-athletes may have had a higher rate of *sensing* than non-athletes (who were higher on *intuition*) because many competitive athletes live "in the moment" to achieve success in their personal sport. In relationship to extraversion and introversion, of the 48 non-athletes, 60% scored as extraverts, and more notably, of the 43 athletes, 70% scored as extroverts, (Reiter, Liput, and Nirmal, 2007).

When looking at the combination of preferences, one out of the 16 types showed noteworthy results. Reiter, Liput, and Nirmal (2007) found that 22% of the participants matched up with the modal type of ENFP (Extraversion-Intuition-Feeling-Perceiving); nine who were athletes, and 11 who were non-athletes. The combination of INFP (Introversion-Intuition-Feeling-Perceiving) was almost three times more common among non-athletes (19%), when compared to athletes (7%). Many of the other combinations were generally equal in percentages when comparing the two groups. Three of the 16 combinations were not endorsed by any of the participants: INTJ (Introversion-iNtuition-Thinking-Judging), ESTP (Extraversion-Sensing-Thinking-Perceiving), and ENTJ (Extraversion-iNtuition-Thinking-Judging), (Reiter, Liput, and Nirmal's 2007).

Table 2
MBTI

16 Preference Types			
ISTJ	ISFJ	INFJ	INTJ
ISTP	ISFP	INFP	INTP
ESTP	ESFP	ENFP	ENTP
ESTJ	ESFJ	ENFJ	ENTJ

How do African American Male student-athletes Develop Their Learning Styles?

According to Banks (2005), how a male African American student-athlete develops his learning styles is reflective of how he develops the habit of mental self-management academically as well as athletically. Mental self-management habits include the student-athlete having his learning style identified, his learning how to monitor and improve his learning skills, his using different learning environments that compliment his learning style, and trying to learn to complete the learning cycle based on his learning style.

Banks (2005) contended that if the African American student-athlete has not learned self-management habits before entering college, this should be a part of his learning style development. Self-management is also known as metacognition and is the art of planning, monitoring, and evaluating the learning process. For an African American student-athlete to be successful at establishing solid self-management habits, he would have become aware of his psycho-social influences. It is at this point that he should also become more cognizant of his balance or lack of balance between athletic identity and academic identity.

Academic identity, athletic identity and identity foreclosure can be strengthened or balanced out during the transitional period to autonomy. *Academic identity* refers to the challenges in the educational development which includes a serious stifling of achievement through barriers of identity, aspiration, and pride created in school systems. *Athletic identity* refers to "the degree to which an individual identifies with the athlete role." *Identity foreclosure* refers to the state of mind an individual has while he is committed to an occupation or ideology without considering or exploring additional options. Both athletic identity (AI) and identity foreclosure (IF) serve as positive attributes for the more gifted athlete but can serve as academic deterrents for the moderately skilled athlete. Also for the gifted athlete, AI and IF prevent him from exploring other gifts he may possess academically.

While looking at the psychosocial and emotional realities of the African American college athlete experience, Mickey C. Melandez (2008), explored the social experiences of a small group of African American football student-athletes attending a predominantly White university in the northeastern United States. A qualitative *grounded theory* methodology was employed for data collection. Analysis and a coding system were created centered on the main areas of team, campus, and city experiences. Melandez's (2008) findings revealed that the African American student-athletes felt isolated, rejected, and mistrustful of their African American and White classmates and teammates. They also felt unfairly judged by their coaches and campus community. Other team, campus, and city issues were revealed, all of which negatively influenced these student-athletes' emotional and educational experiences.

According to Serie McDougal (2009):

The African worldview is characterized by communalism, spirituality, and cooperation, while the dominant European worldview in Western society is characterized by individuality, materialism, and competition for resources. For people of African descent in America, the African worldview is the basis from which African American youth negotiate their way through the influences of the European worldview, racism and social experiences such as education. Because teachers' perceptions, approaches, and expectations of students are shaped by teachers' cultural backgrounds, if they do not enter the classroom culturally prepared (with adequate knowledge of the history and culture of African Americans), they risk misinterpreting students' culture as a deviance or as a disability.

McDougal (2009) conducted her study on what she called the "Afrocentric paradigm." The basic premise of the Afrocentric paradigm is that the culture, experiences and perceptions of people of African descent must be at the center of any human enterprise dealing with people of African descent. She concluded that the findings suggest that many of the students interviewed learn and understand better when teachers provide them with a constant explanation of what they are learning, demonstrative examples of how to do what they are being asked to do, how to apply the concepts that they are learning, and how those concepts, ideas, and information are relevant to their everyday lives. The students had the desire to experience information holistically and to know how it relates to the student-athlete's everyday lives. They responded better to teachers that presented the opportunity to introduce them to problem-based teaching strategies that use real world/real life problems as the focus for teaching problem-solving skills and self-directed learning.

McDougal (2009) noted the male African American student-athlete learning style includes worldview influences. One important influence would be *Ethnic Identity* which develops during adolescence (Phase II). Ethnic identity is the extent to which one identifies with a particular ethnic group. It refers to one's sense of belonging to an ethnic group and the part of one's thinking, perceptions, feelings, and behavior that is due to ethnic group membership. The ethnic group tends to be one in which the individual claims heritage (Phinney, 1996). Ethnic identity is separate from one's personal identity as an individual, although the two may reciprocally influence each other.

The foundation for identity development is rooted in Erickson's 1968 work, *Identity: Youth and Crisis.* Adolescence is the fifth stage of development in Erickson's theory, and occurs between the ages of 12 to 18 years old. This is the ego stage of development when the child learns identity role versus role confusion. This is the stage when peer groups are developed and role models are found. For the African American male student-athlete, this is when he learns to shine in his own light as an athlete or learn to share the light with his team. This is also when the fork in the road can separate academics and athletics priorities. This research contends that Ethnic Identity, Athletic Identity, Academic Identity, and Identity Foreclosure begin to develop and solidify themselves in the male African American student-athlete during the fifth stage of development.

According to Erickson (1968), the identity crisis of adolescence is resolved by reconciling the identities imposed upon oneself by one's family and society with one's need to assert control and seek out an identity that brings one satisfaction, feelings of industry, and competence. During adolescence, according to French, Seidman, Allen, and Aber (2006), the development of ethnic identity is as critical facet, particularly for adolescences of color. For a student-athlete, the development of athletic identity and identity foreclosure is critical to a professional athlete hopeful. However, a mature student-athlete will learn how to find balance in the two and be able to integrate academic identity and balance in his undertaking. The male African American student-athlete struggles to find autonomy as he endeavors to learn an alternative career. According to Harrison and Lawrence (2003) budding athletes spend extensive hours in athletic practices, but fail to examine different roles, and the perception that one's career is unaffected by one's actions are associated with lower self-efficacy for career decision making. Murphy, Petitpas, Brewer, & Van Raalte (1996) concluded that this behavior is associated with race/ethnicity, athletic identity, and the relationship to individual, environmental, and social differences.

According to Tara Orchard (2011), a student-athlete must be physically and mentally prepared to arrive on game day feeling confident in the ability to perform. He must also learn how to adjust during that game should things begin to spiral out of control? The male African American college student-athlete who is the least successful in college may also struggle with adjusting his mental attitude on game day. Orchard (2011) observed that when the momentum in the performance changes on game day, and all the proper preparations have been undertaken, the student-athlete's ability to manage the mental impact of that moment is the key to turning the momentum back around. A primary aspect of student-athlete's ability to mentally perform under pressure includes their ability to process information during times of stress. Orchard (2011) asserted that the student-athlete's personality type can have a profound impact on how he reacts to stress and move forward in the moment.

Orchard (2011) also reviewed MTBI personalities reporting that an athlete spends a significant amount of time learning, gathering data, refining his skills and understanding his game. She noted that his personality type plays a role in how he approaches learning. If a student-athlete understands his natural preference for learning, he will be able to find ways to enhance his ability to gather and learn information. She contends that even though student-athletes may be both sensors and intuitive, there is a good chance that most young student-athletes, will have a strong tendency to perform as a Sensor (S). That is because often as a young person, especially an athlete, he is in a position where he is being trained to learn physical skills by breaking them down into their component parts and building up as he goes. As a result, even if he is naturally an Intuitive (N), he may learn to adapt and function as a Sensor. A Sensor naturally wants to jump in and just do it while an Intuitive is more likely to step back and think about it.

According to Orchard (2011), during times of stress one's natural tendency is to behave as an S or N may escape. The S may try hard to figure out the big picture of what is going on while the N may try to focus on the mechanics and details of the situation. The problem is, if one were well trained and knowledgeable prior to the game changing moment and then you begin stepping out of one's natural tendency, the result is putting oneself into a questioning frame of mind. Once questioning begins, confidence starts to decline, and the momentum runs further and further away.

Orchard (2011) states, "The key to managing your psychological reaction to a change in momentum is understanding your natural strengths and seeking information that you need, in that moment, to regain your well-trained footing. You want to ask the questions you need based on how you need to process information."

How Do the African American Student-Athletes Apply Their Learning Styles to Motivation and Their Perception of Being Successful in College?

Banks (2005) concluded that the result of a male African American student-athlete's psychosocial development becomes most evident once the athlete begins college. Many arrive to college still in the adolescent stage of development where fidelity is still an issue in their lives. If the male African American student-athlete has not resolved his racial/ethnic identity by this point, he will continue to wrestle with the problem as he transitions into Erickson's stage six, young adult. Bank addresses other psychosocial challenges that the student-athlete continues to form a sense of self to include role conflict, isolation, autonomy, academic concerns, interpersonal relationships, and injuries.

William Cross (1971) developed a model of the racial identity stages, which he referred to as "nigrescence" and defined it as a resocialization experience in which a healthy African American progresses from a non-Afrocentric to an Afrocentric to a multicultural identity. Cross developed his model with the goal of outlining racial identity as a dynamic progression, as influenced by those in a particular individual's ethnic group as well as those outside it, and acknowledging ethnocentric and multicultural frames. The Nigrescence process has been suggested to be part of becoming an adult. For the male African American student-athlete, where he is positioned in the Nigrescence scale process can also affect his learning style (1971).

The primary learning style for the male African American student-athlete appears to be kinesthetic, factoring in Gardner's Theory of Multiple Intelligences (1983) into learning style development. Gardner (1993) differentiated between intelligence and learning styles by describing a style as "a general approach that an individual can apply equally to an indefinite range of content" (pp. 83-84). He defined learning styles as being equivalent to the definition of an Approach to Learning as proposed by Bowles (2004). Approaches to Learning are the ways that people acquire and maintain their intelligence while talents are the ways in which intelligence is expressed (Bowles, 2004). Gardner defines intelligence as, the ability to solve problems, or to create products, that are valued within one or more cultural settings (Gardner, 1983/2003) He maintained that it is important to ascertain the empirical linkages between learning styles and their association with specific intelligences. The intelligences Gardner developed are:

1. Linguistic Intelligence: the capacity to use language to express what's on your mind and to understand other people. Any kind of writer, orator, speaker, lawyer, or other person for whom language is an important stock in trade has great linguistic intelligence.
2. Logical/Mathematical Intelligence: the capacity to understand the underlying principles of some kind of causal system, the way a scientist or a logician does; or to manipulate numbers, quantities, and operations, the way a mathematician does.
3. Musical Rhythmic Intelligence: The capacities to think in music; to be able to hear patterns, recognize them, and perhaps manipulate them. People who have strong musical intelligence don't just remember music easily, they can't get it out of their minds, and it's so omnipresent.
4. Bodily/Kinesthetic Intelligence: the capacity to use your whole body or parts of your body (your hands, your fingers, your arms) to solve a problem, make something, or put on some kind of production. The most evident examples are people in athletics or the performing arts, particularly dancing or acting.
5. Spatial Intelligence: the ability to represent the spatial world internally in your mind—the way a sailor or airplane pilot navigates the large spatial world, or the way a chess student-athlete or sculptor represents a more circumscribed spatial world. Spatial intelligence can be used in the arts or in the sciences.
6. Naturalist Intelligence: the ability to discriminate among living things (plants, animals) and sensitivity to other features of the natural world (clouds, rock configurations). This ability was clearly of value in our evolutionary past as hunters, gatherers, and farmers; it continues to be central in such roles as botanist or chef.
7. Intrapersonal Intelligence: having an understanding of yourself; knowing who you are, what you can do, what you want to do, how you react to things, which things to avoid, and which things to gravitate toward. We are drawn to people who have a good understanding of themselves. They tend to know what they can and can't do, and to know where to go if they need help.

8. Interpersonal Intelligence: the ability to understand other people. It's an ability we all need, but is especially important for teachers, clinicians, salespersons, or politicians— anybody who deals with other people.
9. Existential Intelligence: the ability and proclivity to pose (and ponder) questions about life, death, and ultimate realities.

For the male African American student-athlete, areas to examine may include the linkage between his holistic (conceptual) learning style and kinesthetic intelligence.

There are many encounters of developmental tasks that will eventually foster the male African American student-athlete's emotional welfare and development. Parham (1993) identified these tasks to include the broadening and enhancing of individual skills that will master his environment, learning to be an individual within one's family and community, teaching him how to strengthen close relationships, helping him to align his moral and ethical standards with his beliefs and goals, and helping him to find a career goal that is self-rewarding.

There are two forms of motivation to be considered when looking at the learning styles of the male African American college student-athlete. *External motivation,* sources outside of oneself that motivates a person. *Internal motivation,* the need to accomplish goals comes from within oneself. According to Banks (2005), much of the external motivational support for the male African American student-athlete comes from the coaches in the college athletic department. These influences complicate the student-athlete's ability to achieve internal motivation.

The male African American college student-athlete like other males students of color, come from various cultural backgrounds. Historically, male students of color, regardless of their race, have found themselves facing similar challenges during the college experience. Molly Redden (2011) studied a report released by the College Board in June 2011, entitled *The Educational Experience of Young Men of Color.* It studied 92 male high school and college students across the country who were African American, Native American, Asian-American or Pacific Islander, or Hispanic or Latino, attended high school, four-year colleges, two-year colleges, or nontraditional or for-profit institutions, and varied widely in age. The report found commonality in certain hurdles all of the males encountered. These hurdles were stereotypes, pressures to support their communities or families, money problems, or having a feeling of alienation from their campuses. This report offered several suggestions for improving outreach to the students. According to Redden (2011), colleges with multicultural centers that reach out to students and familiarize them with campus resources tend to have very high retention rates.

Terragrossa, Englander, and Wang (2010) conducted a study and presented the findings in *How Student Achievement is Related to Student Behaviors and Learning Style Preferences.* This study examined the degree to which student behavioral choices (e.g., commitment of energies to alcohol consumption, fitness activities, Internet use, study hours, and employment hours) can be explained by the learning style profiles of those students. The results indicate that for four of the five behavioral variables, the learning style profiles have a significant impact on those variables. They also examined the influence of learning style preferences, student ability and student behavioral choices on performance in introductory microeconomics. This study utilized the restricted least squares regression methodology to evaluate the relative impact on student performance of these three separate categories (each considered as a group) of explanatory variables—student behavioral choices, learning style preferences, and innate student ability. The results indicated that student performance is significantly related to, in order of importance: student ability, behavioral choices and learning style preferences. Inferences are made regarding how the results of this study can be applied by instructors and other university personnel to improve academic performance.

In the Terragrossa, Englander, and Wang study (2010), the Dunn and Dunn Learning Styles Model (DDLSM; Dunn, 2000) was used to measure and explain learning styles. Factor analysis was used to reduce the twenty learning style preference variables of the DDLSM model to five instrumental factors, which then were used to explain variations in the student behavioral choice variables. The *Ordinary Least Squares* estimation approach was applied to a system of equations to examine the influence of behavioral choices, learning style preferences and academic ability on student performance in introductory microeconomics. Data for 125 students were collected from eight sections of the same introductory microeconomics course over four semesters from spring of 2003 through fall of 2005 at a university in the northeast. All sections were taught by the same instructor. The introductory microeconomics course is the first semester of a two-course economics sequence that is required of all business majors.

The conclusion of Terragrossa, Englander, and Wang (2010) was that student achievement is significantly correlated with student's behavioral choices and their learning styles. The findings of their paper, however, suggested that for the student sample examined here, student ability played the most significant role in explaining variations in student performance.

Terragrossa, Englander, and Wang (2010) also believed the results of their research reinforced earlier works published stressed the importance of developing teaching approaches and tools to better accommodate the learning styles of students. The findings also support the analysis of Brooks (2009) who had argued that government efforts to address student dropout behavior and increase graduation rates would be advanced by offering greater support to and adopting the teaching strategies of community colleges, because they have recognized the importance of student learning styles and have therefore made greater efforts to accommodate pedagogy to these various learning styles.

The implication of the Terragrossa, Englander, and Wang (2010) study was that colleges and universities may play some role in influencing student behavioral choices. However, it may be ironic that while a substantial majority of colleges and universities maintain counseling programs, residence hall staff and campus security efforts to discourage students from alcohol consumption, student performance in this study was found to be more threatened by excessive fitness activities and employment hours. The student counseling staff at the university from which the student subjects of this study were drawn reported that there were considerably more resources at that institution, and the vast majority of other higher education institutions are committed to addressing the problem of student alcohol use than the problems introduced by poor student time management skills which may lead to poor student academic performance.

Terragrossa, Englander, and Wang's (2010) assessment concluded that college athletic departments and the NCAA may need to consider whether current schedules make a mockery of the term student-athlete. Just as student counseling services are routinely advising students against the harm that alcohol and drugs may be doing, these counseling professionals may need to put more emphasis on the temperance-related benefits of time management skills.

This study by Terragrossa, Englander, and Wang (2010) did not specifically factor in the male African American college football student-athlete. And in their limitations they addressed the fact that they had difficulty learning the representativeness of the students.

Reading and Motivation

Clara Taylor (2005) conducted a study examining what motivated the African- American middle grade male to read. She was exploring why some African American males are more successful academically than others in reading. Taylor investigated possible barriers that are interconnected and relate to reading achievement and reading motivation. She used critical narrative inquiry and the theoretical lens of critical race theory for her research. This was a qualitative analysis which concurrently investigated racial/ethnic identity relative to the background, popular culture, and learning styles as being motivational factors when engaging African American males in the reading and learning process. There were six African American male participants in this study. There were two from the 6th grade, two from the seventh, and two from the eighth grade. All of the students attended the Martin Luther King, Jr. Middle School, under the Atlanta Public School System.

Taylor (2005) had each student complete a reading interest inventory, online learning styles assessment, and an interview. The criterion for participation was: low social economic challenges (SEC) status, determined by free or reduced school lunch enrollment. The students also had to obtain a certain score on the Georgia Criterion Reference Competence Test (CRCT). Three students (one each from grades –6-8) scored in the 349 or higher range, representing the 60th percentile or higher. The other three students (one each from grades 6-8) received scores of 299 or less, representing the 35th percentile or lower range.

After the data for Taylor's (2005) study was coded, several themes emerged. To facilitate comparison, the themes were categorized as: (a) Attitudes, habits, and perceptions about reading and education, (b) Gender identity and peer identity (c) Family expectations and teacher expectations, (d) Popular culture interests, (e) Textbooks, and (f) Learning styles and teaching styles. Analyzing these themes in the different stories of these participants attempted to provide a glimpse into what motivates low-achieving and high-achieving African American males to read. This cross-case analysis compare students within grade levels and across grade levels and simultaneously compared students within identified reading levels (low achievers to low achievers and high achievers to high achievers) and across reading levels (low achievers to high achievers).

According to Taylor (2005), the study addressed the two major questions:

A. "What cultural influences that facilitate or diminish the personal reading motivation are revealed in the stories of middle-grade African American males' experiences in reading?"

B. "How is the motivation to read revealed in personal stories of high- and low-achieving African American middle grade males?"

Among the findings, the race of the teacher was considered. The student participants, Jermaine, Que, Kobe, Rico, Tae, and Trae revealed experiences both negative and positive about previous reading teachers. Taylor reported that the students have had teachers of their same race (African American), differential racial background and ethnicity during their educational experience. After interviewing all of the students, the teacher's race did not appear to be a factor in facilitating or diminishing reading motivation of the six students.

Taylor (2005) stated that Kunjufu (2002) implied that the most significant characteristic of Master Teachers is not their race or gender but the expectations they have of their students. Teachers need to make students learn. She also reported that Kunjufu (2002) maintained that effective education for the African American students must include infiltration of the power of the peer. Peer pressure is the major influence on African American youth.

Taylor (2005) noted, African American males in particular turn to their peers for approval in nonacademic ways. African American males develop "coolness" and style of movement, speech, and dress based on the influences of the street success of neighborhood men. She introduced another theory - that African Americans develop a sense of collective identity in opposition to the social identity of white Americans (Lundy, 2003). Academic success for the male African American is often perceived as "acting White" and is negatively sanctioned by many neighborhood peers. Acting white is based on the premise that learning in school is considered a white cultural practice seen as (a) taking away from their own cultural identity, (b) abandoning the norms of their peers, and (c) rejecting their peer group.

In Taylor's study, she provided detailed accounts of her interviews with each of the students. For the student, Kobe, she highlighted his need to encourage other male African Americans to be successful readers by his goal to write a book about African American history. She compared it to her study to Perry, Steele, & Hilliard (2003) entitled Young, Gifted, and African American: Promoting High Achievement Among African American Students. Their goal was to help readers get a sense of the content and power of the African American philosophy of schooling by writing a close reading of seven African American narratives. The overall goal was to make clear the feelings, meanings, and significance of African Americans and how they relate to their schooling and learning process. Perry, Steele, & Hilliard (2003) wanted it to show how the philosophy of education is associated with African Americans. The narratives provided real life accounts and stories that sustained and could continue sustaining the desire for learning in a people for whom educational accomplishment was not necessarily linked to comparable rewards (Perry, Steele, & Hilliard, 2003).

Taylor (2005) reported that many of the students spoke about being bored in the classroom and reading boring materials as challenges and turn offs for them that may be responsible for diminished reading motivation. She refers to Kunjufu (2002), who suggests one way to fight boredom for African American students is to create a curriculum that mirrors the student. Kunjufu contends that students should be taught to understand the difference between African and Negro history; and taught that the acquisition of skills is not designed for their personal enhancement but are to be returned to the community for its empowerment.

Taylor (2005) states that students must be connected to their history. The findings of this study suggest that cultural influences are important to consider in the reading curriculum and instructional practices of African American males. She reported that the key to unlocking the genius of African American children would require tapping into the talent bank found in the relationship of curriculum to cultural identity. She reported a study of the relationship of ethnicity, race, and culture to curriculum was conducted by Edelin (1995) that found the relationship may become more revealing as urban education continues to be examined. Taylor also reported that it is imperative that curriculum theorizing must adopt an understanding of curriculum as a racial text to address the many needs of a diverse school population.

Taylor (2005) presented Marzano, Pickering, and Pollock (2001) and their theory that reinforcing effort can help teach students one of the most valuable lessons they can learn, the harder you try, the more successful you are. They stated teachers need to believe in the students' ability to be successful, and this must be communicated genuinely from teacher to student. As discussed earlier in this study, male African Americans are too often placed in special education classes for have learning styles that go against the norm.

Taylor (2005) found learning styles and teaching styles were different for each student. While Que was a visual learner, Kobe, and Tay were tactile learners who also preferred lecturing (auditory learning). All three low-achieving (Jermaine, Rico, & Trae) students were primarily tactile learners, which is consistent with the theory presented by Jackson-Allen and Christenberry (1994) research findings also supported the idea that low achievers had a stronger preference for learning experiences that involve opportunities for mobility. The tactile learner may have problems in a reading classroom unless the teacher designs learning activities that involve mobility. Jackson-Allen and Christenberry also suggested that young African American males who are identified as either low or high achievers are more alike than they are different in their preferences for various learning modalities were supported in this research. While all the participants had teachers with different teaching styles, many of the teachers' styles matched the students' learning styles. This research will seek to find whether the male African American college football student-athlete show the same commonalities.

Taylor compared the low-achieving to the high-achieving students, and did not find a noticeable difference in their stories. The attitudes and success stories about reading appeared to begin before these students reached middle school. Taylor (2005) concludes her study with the concern about how reading/education relates to identity formation of African American males. She quotes the statements by Hale (2001) as accurately addressing this concern:

> The boy is father to the man. It is my opinion that we ignore the needs of African American boys in early childhood, the time when the foundation for later achievement is laid. By the time alarming problems arise, in adolescence, prospects are more difficult to reverse . . .. Academic failure is not an accident. Academic failure, incarceration, and unemployment are outcomes of public schooling for African American boys. More African American males between the ages of eighteen and twenty-two are in prison today than enrolled in

college .... African American males have the lowest grade point average and the lowest scores on standardized tests. Twenty-three million Americans are functionally illiterate, and the largest proportions of these are African American males. Unemployment for African American males between the ages of 15 and 35 is 50%...Most African American children, particularly African American males, do not like school. Many drop out intellectually by the time they are in the fifth grade and make it legal at the age of 16. There is no doubt in my mind that if this snapshot were representative of White males, there would be a declaration of a national epidemic. As a result, major changes would be forced to take place in curriculum design, the instructional process, and the educational process (pp. 41-43).

The Interest Convergence Principle

Interest convergence is defined as an act of interest in African Americans achieving racial equality based on the accommodation being provided only when it converges with the interests of whites. Derrick Bell (1992b) stated that when examining the education of the African American, rather than focusing on racial balance, one should focus on obtaining real educational effectiveness, which may entail the improvement of presently desegregated schools as well as the creation or preservation of model African American schools. Bell's argument was a part of his review of the aftermath of the Brown versus The Board of Education court case and interest-convergence.

Jamal Donner (2005) wrote an article for the purpose of "advancing Derrick Bell's (1992b) interest-convergence principle as an analytical lens for understanding the complex role of race in the educational experiences of African American football student-athletes." Donner concluded his article with a discussion of the interest-convergence principle as a means of investigating and establishing alternative strategies on behalf of the student-athlete in order to improve his educational experience and academic outcomes.

Shaun R. Harper (2009) in his article *Race, Interest Convergence, and Transfer Outcomes for African American Male student-athletes,* he uses the *Critical Race Theory* to consider the educational outcomes of African American male student-athletes when transferred to four-year colleges. While his research has been almost exclusively concerned with student-athletes at four-year colleges and universities, and mostly at the National Collegiate Athletic Association's (NCAA) Division I competition level, he purported that previous studies on African American male student-athletes at four-year institutions mostly described racial differences in educational outcomes between them and their white male teammates. In his analysis of graduation rate data from the NCAA, Harper (2006) found the following results:

> That across four cohorts of college student-athletes 47 percent of African American men graduated within six years, compared to 60 percent of white males and 62 percent of student-athletes overall. The averages across four cohorts of basketball student-athletes were 39 percent and 52 percent for African American men and white men, respectively. Forty-seven percent of African American male football student-athletes graduated within six years, compared to 63 percent of their white teammates. Harper's findings led to this conclusion: "Perhaps nowhere in higher education is the disenfranchisement of African American male students more insidious than in college athletics." (p. 6)

In his later research, Harper (2009) incorporated these results through a discussion that racial gaps in degree attainment have occurred for some time. He also recounted that more than 25 years ago, Edwards (1984) discussed his observation about African American sports participants. Edwards stressed the complicated burdens of African American athletes as being psychosocial in that they are confronted with the social stereotypes such as the traditional dumb jock caricature in addition to the racial myth of innate African American athletic superiority, and the added stereotype of the dumb Negro. The male African American student-athlete enters college condemned by racial heritage to intellectual inferiority. According to Harper (2009), it has been found that many African American males are socialized to prioritize sports over academics when they are in high school, and the messages are sustained and amplified once they enroll in college. Harper (2009) reported in the *Chronicle of Higher Education* article entitled "African American Athletes and White Professors: A Twilight Zone of Uncertainty," African American male student-athletes reported feeling that they were not taken seriously by many of their white professors (Perlmutter, 2003).

Harper (2009) asserted the Critical Race Theory (CRT) and how it challenges misconceptions regarding colorblindness, merit, and racial equity; critiques the presumed innocence of self-proclaimed white liberals; and ignites consciousness that leads to social justice and advances for people of color. He refers to Donnor (2005), and his assessment of CRT as offering a useful lens which allows one to see more clearly the contradicting variables create a strong fan base support for success on the football field and but creates a weak supportive fan base for success in the classroom.

Harper (2009) defines Interest Convergence, as those in the majority who enact social, political, and economic change on behalf of minorities rarely do so without first identifying the personal costs and gains associated with such actions.

Donnor (2005) indicates that the African American male who participate in sports are more likely to possess aspirations for pursuing sports professionally than their white counterparts because they believe they will be treated fairly. As a result, African American males will generally interpret their involvement in intercollegiate (and interscholastic) sports as a conduit for achieving their career aspirations (p. 48). Male African American community college football student-athletes set goals to transfer to a four year college based on such career aspirations.

As a result of transfer-oriented goals, many male African American student-athlete football student-athletes end up ineligible or insufficiently prepared to transfer to a four year college because they lack of academic structure, financial support, or lack accurate information about the transfer process. According to Harper (2009) only a small proportion of community college students who intend to transfer to a four-year institution actually do so.

National Collegiate Athletic Association (NCAA) and Male student-athletes

According to the NCAA website for 2011, member colleges and universities have adopted a comprehensive academic reform package designed to improve the academic success and graduation of all student-athletes. The primary operative of the academic reform package is the development of a new academic measurement for sports teams, known as the Academic Progress Rate, or APR. A secondary operative is to penalize sports teams who do not increase the graduation success rate (GSR) of their student-athletes. The new reform has been implemented since 2004 and appears to be affective in diminishing the overall problem of student-athlete retention and graduation as a whole.

On May 24, 2011, the NCAA reported on their website that "academic scorecards keep improving." They announced that reform movements are shifting to "automatic expectation" of student-athlete success. According to the most recent figures, the latest four-year Division I Academic Progress Rate is 970, up three points over last year. The average four-year rate also rose in the high-profile sports of men's basketball, football and baseball (Hosick, 2011), sports that are most represented by African American males.

According to the NCAA website (2011), President Mark Emmert has stated that, "For the first time in history of intercollegiate sport, we have a common language and common expectation around academics," Emmert said. "The expectation is that every program will reach a certain level of academic performance, and that level is important. To this end, the reform effort has been almost immeasurable in its impact," (NCAA.org, 2011).

On December 8, 2010, the NCAA reported releasing stunning information. They had been tracking student-athlete ethnicity for the past 11 years. They have now discovered that the male African American comprises the highest percentage of football student-athletes across the nation. Per the NCAA release, 45.8% of student-athletes in Division I football (including the Football Bowl Subdivision and the Football Championship Subdivision) were African American, followed closely by White football student-athletes at 45.1 percent. The NCAA proclaim that this is the first time that African Americans have been the dominant demographic in all of Division I football.

In a May 24, 2011 release by the NCAA, **Michelle Brutlag Hosick** reported that the 2011 release of Academic Progress Rate data revealed that Historically African American Colleges and Universities continue to struggle with the academic metric that measures the eligibility and retention of student-athletes at a team level. Where many non-HBCU peers— including schools with similarly limited resources— show some improvement, teams at HBCUs are trending in the opposite direction.

The NCAA has committed to working with Historically African American Colleges and Universities to improve their academic performance. Looking to the future, the Division I membership is examining how to further strengthen academics in a number of ways, said Walter Harrison, president of the University of Hartford and chair of the Division I Committee on Academic Performance.

For the 2009-10 APR reporting year (the data released in May 2011), 33 of the 103 penalties issued by the NCAA went to teams at historically African American institutions. HBCU advocates say the reasons for the downward movement are complex and extend beyond a lack of resources, though that factor is cited most often as a reason for poor academic performance. They report that many institutions with more funding can hire academic advisors, tutors and other people to ensure their student-athletes go to class, many HBCUs just don't have usually have access to the same funding.

The primary objective of this study was to use naturalistic inquiry, a type of phemonalogical study, to create a more in-depth understanding of the basic learning styles of the male African American college football student-athlete that would add to the current pool of knowledge available to researchers. It endeavored to discover the student-athlete's belief of his learning style and how his perception of such style has motivated his career decision-making. Learning styles of the African American male college football athlete has not been adequately explored (Harrison & Lawrence, 2010). A thorough understanding of the African American college football athlete's learning style will help to establish the intensity of the psychological impact it has on his motivation to make sound career decisions.

The method chosen for this study was qualitative. By conducting a one-on-one exploratory naturalistic interview with three male African American football student- athletes.

Qualitative research is used to gain insight into the male African American football student-athletes' attitudes, behaviors, value systems, concerns, motivations, aspirations, culture or lifestyles. Focus groups, in-depth interviews, content analysis, ethnography, evaluation and semiotics are among the many formal approaches that are used for qualitative research which also involves the analysis of any unstructured material, including feedback forms, reports or media clips (QSR International Pty Ltd, 2011).

Quantitative research was not chosen for this study because the goal was not to measure the reactions of the participants rather than, comparing any groups, nor seeking to aggregate the data collected.

This research is looking for details and data that creates important categories and dimensions of learning style preferences of the male African American football student-athlete. Qualitative case studies can produce a baseline of study that can then develop into a larger quantitative research project that determines the extent of the qualitative findings and its validity when applied to a larger sample of the same focus group.

While this study focused primarily on the phenomenological theory of the learning styles of the male African American college student-athlete resulting in motivation, it also explored how the African American learning styles impact his motivation and his perception of career decision-making. Phenomenological qualitative research provided an opportunity to discuss the personal experiences of the African American male college football athlete as he was willing to disclose his thoughts, feelings, and memories.

Data Collection and Fieldwork Strategies

The data collection methods used for this research was interviews and observation. Using the snowball approach, referrals for participants were contacted by the researcher either by email or telephone to recruit voluntary participation for this study. The researcher contacted one or two persons known to her to be a NCAA Division I male African American football student-athlete. The study was explained to the prospective participants. Confidentiality was discussed. After the subjects consented to participate in the study, the participants were mailed a letter of participation, an opt in/opt out letter, and an informed consent form prior to being scheduled for an interview. The anticipated sample size for this study was 20 male African American football student-athletes. Each participant was to be interviewed one time with an expected interview to last for one hour maximum. All interviews were conductive using objective questioning. The interviews were conducted in conversation style.

To implement the snowball sampling, the researcher asked the participants to refer other possible participants who would represent the population of study. If they had persons who they believe may be interested in participating in this study, the participant provided the researcher with the contact information needed for the potential participant. Other people in the community, including the social network and college coaches also were asked to refer student-athletes. Each of the additional participants were contacted by telephone or mail to recruit for participation and provided with the same information as the previous participants. Snowballed participants received the snowballing letter in addition to a letter of recruitment. All participants signed letters of informed consent and letters to opt in/opt out for record keeping purposes in the study.

The qualitative data collected was based on the response of the participants and the degree to which all of the participants were willing to be honest and clear about their experiences. Open-ended questions relative to the male African American college student-athlete's sports and academic experiences were used. Semi-structured, practical, and in-depth questions were asked that apply to the current issues affecting the student-athlete's college experience.

Open-ended questions, according to Michael Patton (2002), provide longer, more detailed, and varied content in the responses. The analysis of open-ended questions is more difficult because the responses are neither systematic nor standardized. These questions also permit the researcher to understand the world as seen by the respondents. Questions of this style also permit the researcher to provide a better visual of the world of the college student-athlete as they see it (2002).

Observation was an important fieldwork strategy for this research. It allowed the researcher to better understand the complexity of the student-athlete, if what he considers as his learning style is reflective of his perception in college. Observation, using empathic neutrality and mindfulness, included a minimal participation in some of the activities of the participants by the researcher. Participant observation data collection, according to Patton (2002), permits the evaluation researcher to understand a program or treatment to an extent not entirely possible using only the insights of others obtained through interviews.

Population and Sampling

There are two forms of sampling, probability and non-probability. According to the University of California, Davis (UC Davis, 2006), probability samples are selected in such a way as to be **representative** of the population. They provide the most valid or credible results because they reflect the characteristics of the population from which they are selected (e.g., residents of a particular community and students at an elementary school). Probability samples are either random or stratified.

Probability Sampling

Random Sampling - **Random** sampling gives e**ach individual in the population of interest an equal likelihood of selection.** The key to random selection is that there is no bias involved in the selection of the sample. Any variation between the sample characteristics and the population characteristics is only a matter of chance (UC Davis, 2006).

Stratified Sampling: A stratified sample is a mini-reproduction of the population. Before sampling, the population is divided into characteristics of importance for the research. For example, by gender, social class, education level, and religion. Then the population is randomly sampled *within* each category or stratum. Stratified samples are as good as or better than random samples, but they require fairly detailed advance knowledge of the population characteristics, and therefore are more difficult to construct (UC Davis, 2006).

Non-Probability Sampling

Non-probability samples are less desirable than probability samples; however, a researcher may not be able to obtain a random or stratified sample, or it may be too expensive. A researcher primary motive may not be about generalizing his/her results to a larger population. The validity of non-probability samples can be increased by trying to approximate random selection, and by eliminating as many sources of bias as possible (UC Davis, 2006).

According to UC Davis (2006), there are two types of non-probability samples quota and purposive. They are:

- **Quota sampling**: When the researcher deliberately sets the proportions of levels or strata within the sample. The researcher sets a quota, independent of population characteristics.
- **P**urposive sampling: A non-representative subset of some larger population, and is constructed to serve a very specific need or purpose. The researcher will attempt to zero in on the target group, interviewing whoever is available. Subsets of a purposive sample are **snowball sample and convenience sample.**
    - A snowball sample is achieved by asking a participant to suggest someone else who might be willing or appropriate for the study. Snowball samples are particularly useful in hard-to-track populations, such as truants, drug users, etc.
    - A **convenience sample** is a matter of taking what you can get. It is an **accidental** sample. Although selection may be unguided, it probably is not random, using the correct definition of everyone in the population having an equal chance of being selected. Volunteers would constitute a convenience sample.

Sampling Used for This Research

A non-probable, purposive sampling, using snowball sampling was used for this research. Using this selection provided a better access to the focus group of male African American student-athletes available for this study.

The proposed sample group included male African American football student-athletes from a Division I level of the National College Athletic Association (NCAA). By using a non-probability method of sampling it was be easier to locate participants.

Participant Eligibility

Eligibility for participants was based on the college football athlete having played the sport for at least two years while in college. The population for this study was male African American, college football student-athletes between the ages of 18 to 25. The goal of this study was to recruit participants from the NCAA Division I college conferences with the hope of ensuring a high degree of representation of the target population.

According to Patton (2002) there are no rules for sample size in qualitative inquiry. He reports that,

"The validity, meaningfulness, and insights generated from qualitative inquiry have more to do with the information richness of the cases selected and the observable/analytical capabilities of the researcher than with sample size."

In order to obtain some consistency in the findings of this research, the anticipated sample size for this study was twenty (20) participants. It was anticipated that adequate variation in college conferences under the NCAA would be represented among the group of twenty (20); however, this researcher was unable to find enough participants to fulfill the sample goal for this study due to problems with accessibility and availability. It was discovered that interviewing current football athletes may place them at risk of NCAA violations. It also was discovered that those that are no longer playing football are not readily available because of busy life schedules.

The sample size of twenty (20) was based on the DePaulo (2000) Probability of Missing Population Subgroup in a Random Sample table (see Appendix A). DePaulo (2000) developed a table for qualitative research that can be used to assure that the research is accomplishing the goals of the research. It stated that this table is developed to accomplish the objective of qualitative research (reduce the chances of discover failure) versus the goal of quantitative research (to reduce the estimation error). The table is based on calculated probabilities that a subgroup may be missed based on the sample size. For the sample size chosen for this research, twenty (20), the risk factor would have been 0.122 or 12.2%. This means that the probability of missing a subgroup during this research study would have been 12%. This presents as being high; however, this is a pure research study, and the sample size was chosen based on time, availability of the participants, and the available budget for this research.

DePaulo's (2000) Probability of Missing a Population Subgroup in a Random Sample presents the smallest sample size as being 10. Based on DePaulo's (2000) sample size of 10, the population incidence is .349 when looking for 10% representation of the focus group. This means that the probability of a study missing a subgroup by 10% during a research study is 34.9 or 35%. A sample size of three represents the risk of missing a subgroup by 10% is more than 35%.

Thirty-five percent is high; however, this is a pure research study and the sample size was the results of time, availability of the participants, and the available budget for research.

Research Question Guideline

In order to conduct a semi-structured interview, pre-planned questions were used to guide the interviews. Below are the questions used:

- Is football the only important thing in your life?
- How do you think other people would describe you?
- What are your goals in life?
- Are you currently playing football?
- Do you know what learning styles are?
- What do you believe is your learning style?
- How do you see yourself as a student-athlete?
- How do you think you apply your learning style to being a student-athlete?
- Are you in college now?
- What do you know about the history of the male African American football college student-athlete?
- Tell me what I would see if I walked around in your world?
- If you had the opportunity to prepare for college again, what would you do differently? What would change because of it?

Data Collection

Personal interviews using the sensitizing concept were used for the convenience of data collection in the interest of resource limitations. The sensitizing concept originated with Blumer (1954), the late American sociologist, who contrasted definitive concepts with sensitizing concepts. Blumer explained,

> A definitive concept refers precisely to what is common to a class of objects, by the aid of a clear definition in terms of attributes or fixed bench marks. A sensitizing concept lacks such specification of attributes or bench marks and consequently it does not enable the user to move directly to the instance and its relevant content. Instead, it gives the user a general sense of reference and guidance in approaching empirical instances. Whereas definitive concepts provide prescriptions of what to see, sensitizing concepts merely suggest directions along which to look. (p. 7)

While the style of interviewing was informal conversation, a general interview guide approach was incorporated into each interview to cover relevant topics that required exploring during the interview. Patton (2002) reported that an interview guide keeps the interactions focused while allowing individual perspectives and experiences to emerge.

The setting for the interview was at locations conducive to the interviewee. All interviews occurred in their homes. Each interview was scheduled to last for approximately one hour. The outcomes of the interviews' timelines were approximately thirty (30) minutes. The disclosure of confidential information from the participant served as a critical element in the data collection.

Observation for the researcher as a participant/observer was minimal, while acting in the role of a perspective outsider. Inquiries were one-on-one interviews which focused on obtaining clear data. The duration of the research did not exceed 6 months for data collection. The focus of this research was from a holistic perspective, exploring how varied data comes together to develop valid information.

The primary data collection methods used for this research was audio recording and phenomenological interviewing. Audio recording allowed the interview to be transcribed for better interpretation. Planned video recording was to allow for discovery of nonverbal behavior and communication such as facial expressions, gestures, and emotions. Audio and video recording were planned to be used to enhance the outcome of the interview's validity in relationship to nonverbal behaviors related to the participants responses.

The researcher was unable to use video recording due to mechanical difficulties with the video camera. The participants were difficult to locate and time taken out to leave the location and resolve the problems with the video recorder would have compromised the availability of the participants in that they did have a lot of time available to participate.

Phenomenological interviewing is a specific type of in-depth interviewing grounded in a philosophical tradition (Patton, 2002). Phenomenology is the study of lived experiences and the ways we understand those experiences to develop a worldview. It rests on the assumption that there is a structure and essence to shared experiences that can be narrated.

The purpose of this type of interviewing is to describe the meaning of a concept or phenomenon that several individuals share. The primary advantage of phenomenological interviewing is that it permits an explicit focus on the researcher's personal experience combined with those of the interviewees (Smith, 2007).

While being mindful, the research was cognizant of ethical issues that may have risen during the interviews. Before interviewing, care was taken to explain the purpose of the research and allow the participants to ask questions. All participants were required to sign consent forms to participate in the study. Clear lines of communication were established with the participant relative to the goals of this study. Pre-interview discussion with the participants included risk information (if any) that may arise from the interview. The participants understood in advance that his participation is purely voluntary. They were given the option to take breaks or terminate participation at any time that they feel that they are unable to participate with the interview.

The pre-interview discussion included a confidentiality agreement. The difference between confidentiality and anonymity was discussed. All data collected from the interviews will be anonymous. Informed consent was in written form for each participant based on the Institutional Review Board (IRB) guideline requirements. Information provided to the participants was included who has access to all data collected and for what purpose.

Data collection boundaries for this researcher were based on the sensitivity of the data being collected and the emotional response of the participants. This research respected the needs, feelings, and emotions of the participants.

Data Analysis

This research is interpretive and seeks to present a holistic analysis of the data collected. Conducting interpretive research for a better understanding of the social process of the male African American student-athlete involved getting inside the cognitive world of the college student-athlete. The interpretive approach is often used by qualitative researchers in semiotics, deconstructivism, aesthetic criticism, ethnomethodology, and hermeneutics. This study will be using the interpretive approach to explore ethnomethodology (the study of how people interact in ways that maintain the social structure of the situations in which they find themselves).

Miles and Huberman stated that qualitative data analysis consists of "three concurrent flows of activity: data reduction, data display, and conclusion drawing/verification" (1994, p. 10). The data for this study incorporated all of the flows of activity in qualitative analysis to discover how varied data comes together to develop valid information.

The researcher transcribed all of the data collected, found common themes, and drew conclusions from the themes that emerged. Further research was conducted to verify the validity of the theme. The research also looked for any preconceptions and bias found in the interviews that affect his perception of career decision-making. Particular focus was on themes that address commonalities in learning styles and motivation. According to Orlikowski and Baroudi (1991), "The interpretive research approach towards the relationship between theory and practice is that the researcher can never assume a value-neutral stance, and is always implicated in the phenomena being studied."

Interpretative Phenomenological Analysis (IPA) was used to develop a thematic network of common themes drawn from the interview. By using IPA, it offers insights into how a given person, in a given context, makes sense of a given phenomenon (Patton, 2002). IPA is the most appropriate style of analysis for this research because it allowed the study to learn a deeper understanding of the male African American college student-athlete and his learning style preferences. This style also allowed the researcher to analyze the data and to determine whether there are any trends in the participants' responses noting how his perceptions are made.

The overall analysis for this research recognized a unique case orientation and considered such when applying induction and creative synthesis. Every student-athlete must be respected for his experience, a crucial piece to conducting an analysis of the data collected. Having recognized the uniqueness of conducting case studies, the research created data of the details found to determine important patterns, themes, and interrelationships to create a mixture of information.

The voice of the research sought to produce data that is credible, authentic, and trustworthy. It sought to provide a balanced understanding of the world of the male African American student-athlete as he experiences college and all of its complexities. It sought to provide new information about the male African American student-athlete and the necessity for him to be taught academically in a way that is fitting for him while allowing him the full opportunity to be successful in his career choices.

Limitations

A qualitative study provides answers that are subject to criticism and interpretation. Much of the information collected is based on each student-athlete's personal experiences. A sample size of three (3) was the result of this study which is insufficient to generalize the conclusions.

Delimitations

The potential for a large group of participants in this study population seemed adequate. This research was focused on using twenty (20) participants, with the possibility of an increase of participants to at least 30. According to DePablo (2000), thirty (30) participants would reduce the risk of missing a group of experiences to .042 or less than 1%.

Purpose

The purpose of this study is to explore the learning styles of the male African American football student-athlete. It will seek to discover how the male African American college football student-athlete learns how to learn and how his learning style motivates him.

Contents

The results of the data analyses conducted in this study are reported in this chapter. This chapter consists of the following sections: (a) Demographic Information, (b) Data Management, (c) Results of Interviews, and (d) Summary.

Demographics

There were three (3) participants in this study. All of the participants were from a Division 1 college. All of the participants were male African American, ages 18 to 25 years old.

One participant for this study held senior class standing at the time of his participation in the present study and has expectations of receiving his bachelor's degree within a few months. One participant is returning to college as a sophomore with expectations of graduating in a year and a half. The third participant is no longer in college and does not have an expected date to return. During one-on-one interviews, the three participants shared intimate details about their relationships and experiences with college football and their academic journey within a Division 1 college institution.

Data Management

There were a total of three (3) student-athletes interviewed for this research. The goal was to interview twenty (20) Division 1, African American football athletes who lived in different areas of the United States. Request for student-athlete referrals was through telephone calls, the social network, face-to-face contact with coaches, and community persons who had relatives or friends which met the qualifications for this study. All of the attempts netted three (3) males available for interview. The three (3) participants lived out of state, to which the researcher flew to interview them. The following information is a result of the data collected from the student-athletes that made themselves available to be interviewed. All data collected has been kept and maintained in a locked file.

The primary objective of this study was to use naturalistic inquiry to create a more in dept understanding of the basic learning styles of the male African American college football student-athlete that added to the current pool of knowledge available to researchers. The endeavor to discover the student-athlete's belief of his learning styles and how his perception of such style has motivated his career decision-making. A thorough understanding of the African American college football student-athlete's learning style will help to establish the intensity of the psychological impact it has on his motivation to make sound career decisions. The results of this study will be used to further future studies of how the intensity of college sports involvement and the learning style of the male African American can affect career decisions for the student-athlete.

Participant Profiles

This research study involved a total of three (3) African American male participants. Each participant is referred to by a pseudonym in order to protect their true identity.

Abraham: Abraham is a male African American between the ages of 21-25 years old. He is single with no children. He grew up in a small suburban town in Southern California. He graduated from high school in 2006. Abraham attended a Historically African American University (HBU) out of state where he played football for two and a half (2 ½) years. Abraham played the position of corner- back in college. The Division I conference that he played in was the Southwestern Athletic Conference (SWAC). He last played football in 2010. He is no longer in college but still lives out of state. Abraham reports that he is in good general health both mentally and physically.

Martin: Martin is a male African American between the ages of 21-25 years old. He is single with a 3-year-old daughter. He grew up in a small suburban town in Southern California. Martin graduated from high school with high honors (3.8 GPA) in 2006. He was a four year letterman at his high school. Martin is attending a Historically African American University (HBU) out of state where he played football for three (3) years. Martin played the position of quarterback in college. The Division I conference that he played in was the Southwestern Athletic Conference (SWAC). Martin last played football in 2010. He is still in college at the same school and plans to finish college in 2012. Martin reports that he has minor foot pains, and a disfigured finger, but "healthy as an ox otherwise."

John: John is a male African American between the ages 21-25 years old. He is single with a 7-month-old son. Martin grew up in a small suburban town in Southern California. He graduated from high school in 2006. Martin was a four-year letterman at his high school. He attended a Historically African American University (HBU) out of state where he played football for 2 years. He played the position of offensive line backer. The Division 1 conference that he played in was the Southwestern Athletic Conference (SWAC). Martin last played football in 2010. Martin is not in college at this time but plans to return in the fall of 2012. He reports that he is in fair health both physically and mentally.

Interview Narrative and Themes

During individual interviews, several themes emerged that may be interpreted as being instrumentally effective in contributing to the African American males use of his learning styles as a positive contributor to motivation. The interviews presented some uniqueness and similarities. While each participant was able to describe his own experiences, it was obvious that all of the student-athletes made a journey that at some point ended on the same road. The following is the results of the student-athlete experiences that impacted their motivation.

During the interviews, this researcher attempted to relax each of the participants by making small talk first. For each of the participants there was a non-verbal sense that while they were willing to participate in this study, they were pre-occupied with other things. Once this researcher realized that the interview time was a gift, great care was taken to use the time wisely. The longest interview lasted approximately 30 minutes.

The interviews were conducted using the twelve (12) basic guideline questions. Each of the interviews usually opened with asking how long the participants played football. Two of the participants played football most of the lives, averaging 17 years. One participant only played football 6 years. The time played included college football playing time. Below are the participants' responses to the guideline questions.

1. *Is football the only important thing in your life?*

All of the participants were asked about how long they played football and the importance of football in their lives. The two participants who played football the longest, Abraham and Martin, enjoyed the sport the most.

Abraham reported to this researcher that,

I played football since I played Junior All American. I started, I'm gonna say 9, 10 years old. When I was a kid it was, you know, it was something to do. I played, before, I played recreational football. I played football all of the time on the streets, all the time, just to do it.

Martin reported that,

"I been playing football about 16 years, since I was 8 years old. A little while. Junior All American Pop Warner. My first year I was kind of chunky, so I played on line, but I still, I just liked being out there."

The two of them grew up dreaming of being National Football League (NFL) athletes.

Abraham said, "Football to me, it pretty much, ah is everything. If football wasn't there, you know, how would I really survive? I always depended on it." And Martin stated, "I was already in the, all in football, you know? My dream, that was my whole life, eat, sleep, dream, Monday thru Friday, my dream that's what I thought about all of the time."

The third participant, John, played football for a short period of time. John also played a second sport, baseball. It is the sport of baseball that he grew up playing. John stated, "Actually about right now it's not important at all but during the time, me playing the game, it was probably the only thing I was thinking about besides my secondary sport which was baseball.

2. *How do you think other people would describe you?*

This researcher asked each of the participants to describe themselves. Each presented themselves as being hard workers, good, honest, friendly.

John seemed to be proud of people saying he was like a "big teddy bear" but a "beast on the field." He also believed that people would describe him as a "good, honest, and caring person." He believed he was a "good friend."

Abraham stated,

"People would describe me as, that's crazy, say as a leader. Fun, live in the moment type of guy, you know? But, ah, very ah, I could be very talkative I guess. I started noticing as I got older, I was like I could be, you know, if I say something, I could be a debater at times. You know? If I think something is right, I probably gonna stick on it. But if I know I am wrong, I am able to listen also. That's what makes me a cool guy."

Martin stated, "I would describe myself as hardworking and determined. Definitely those two. Fairly, I'm a cool guy, just you know, nice to talk to, well rounded. But pretty much hardworking though.

3. *What are your goals in life?*

Each participant was asked about their goals in life. A reoccurring theme for this group was entrepreneurship. Each of them has plans to make money by being successful through hard work developing private businesses.

Abraham said, "I'm working, trying to get as much money as possible to provide for my business ventures that I want to get into." His primary interest is music, "That's it, working and music." Abraham has great dreams which include building his own village,

> "I want to start, I want to do music. I want to start my own business I want to start my own record company. I'm an entrepreneur. I want to build everything from the ground up. I want to create a whole village.

Martin reported being involve in many businesses and said his business goals include,

> "Right now, ah, right now I have a, I'm working on having a couple of businesses. One is the hair business. I sell hair "Her Hair." And then I also, ah, plan on opening a restaurant, within the next year. So, I like the restaurant industry, that whole thing. I also want to get into real estate, buying and selling, you know, houses and things like that and ah few other things.

John replied that his goals include going into business ventures as well. He stated,

> Overall goals is to have enough money to be able to take care of me and my family, and whoever else that might need some money on the way uh and that's pretty much it. However whichever way I go, of course, I'm an entrepreneur. So I'm trying to get into a little bit of everything. Just to see what's my niche. Currently selling hair, also well I started a little, do photography, got a new camera so, I started doing ah little editing videos, music videos I'm starting to do a little production and I also started selling Nestle products I'm starting to getting a little business started with that.

The goals in each of their lives is to be successful, which would be evident by having a lot of money and wealth. They all want enough money to provide for their family (children, parents, etc.) and other people as well.

4. *Are you currently playing football?*

None of the participants are playing college football right now. All stopped playing in the year 2010. A follow up call was made to the participants for clarification as to why each of them stopped playing football because during the interview, the researcher did not ask the reason why each student-athlete is no longer playing. Two of the participants, Abraham and John, had to stop playing football because of a low grade point average. This also caused them to leave college as well. Martin stopped football due to injuries. In his demographic questionnaire, he stated that he suffers from foot pain and a disfigured finger.

5. *Do you know what learning styles are?*

Each of the participants were asked if they understood the definition of learning styles. Each provided the researcher with their definition.

John described learning styles as,

"I guess just pretty much, everybody has different learning styles. We might see the same things but keep it in your mind a different way. It might stick with you a little better, so everybody is different."

Abraham described learning styles as,

"I mean, what type of style, what how do you learn. The different ways of learning, the different ways of learning. I gotta a way different way of learning.

Martin responded, "Ummmm I prob I heard it before but I'm not really sure of what exactly it entitles."

6. *What do you believe is your learning style?*

The predominate learning style for this group was visual learning.

Martin stated that his learning style is both visual and kinesthetic. He states,

"Yeah visual learner and probably more of like a repetitive learner like the more I do it the better obviously the more you do it the better you get but if I read something and then read it again and probably write it down and read it again I am able to get it as opposed to just seeing it one time. So, I mean probably a little bit of both."

Abraham and John stated that their learning style was visual also.

Abraham expressed, "I gotta a way different way of learning. I use my imagination and figure out how it looks, that's how I learned all of my words." Abraham also received special education classes while in high school where he participated in resource classes. He also stated that his, "attention span is very short sometimes," and "I just bounce around." Abraham also said that he needs to be able to relate to the information in order to learn.

John also stated that he would memorize a lot. He said, "I think I'm more of a visual person." He also stated that "looking at it, my eyes are going to be glued to it, and I'm going to be glued to it."

Learning styles were applied to life through different ways. Abraham uses his learning styles to write his music which he equates to being involve in journalism. Because he has a wondering mind, he is constantly writing music after work until he "passes out." He expressed to the researcher that, "My music is just a way that I will be able to talk to the people. I look at music as a way of journalism. I can tell people how I feel. I can tell people about their situations."

Martin uses his learning styles for school and his business development. His visual learning includes making daily agendas to plan for his day and then following it. He researches the internet for information that will help him in his businesses. He also appears to have chosen a college major that is related to his learning style. Martin disclosed to the researcher, "My major right now is RTF, so it's a lot of hands on stuff, so it's not really a lot of writing. Radio, Television, and Film. So, I'm like real good at, I'm trying to be a movie director."

John tried to use the same learning style he used in high school for college but discovered that it didn't work. Part of his learning style included "cheating" or someone providing the answers to him and he just had to learn the answers.

John was not able to apply his learning style to upper division college and has been also been unable to apply his learning style to life. He is currently searching for answers to how his learning style can be applied in his life. He says, he continues to use his learning style in his everyday life, visual learning."

7. *How do you see yourself as a student-athlete?*

Abraham answered this question by replying, "I felt like you know I missed a lotta things. If I wasn't playing football like right now. Everything was kinda laid out for me in football once I got to the school. In Pop Warner it was cool, like high school. Once I got to high school, it was cool."

He says that, "discipline is the other thing I learned. If I knew what, I knew now, I didn't know, I also say if I wasn't playing football, if I knew what life was all about, it kinda blinded me from life, being on the football field.

Martin replied, "Like I have a little agenda that I'll write and I just, I just do it. I mean, as far as my learning style, I mean, how I apply it to my daily life. I mean, everyday I'm always googling and trying to look up something like learning about this hair, or different, looking up different industries, I need to know about entrepreneurship."

John answered, "School is pretty, well college was kinda hard to learn, for looking. They might have it on there, but they go through, it pretty fast. You can ask a question and try to figure it out, but they not gonna spend too much time on it. It's gonna be you. It's strictly gonna be you. Some after school stuff. Some after class stuff to study, to stay abreast of what's going on."

8. *How do you think you apply your learning styles to being a student-athlete?*
Abraham's answer was,

"I was a, when I was coming up, I had resource classes. I couldn't like people, get done with their test fast. It would mess me up. I couldn't get things. It would take me a little more time. Sometimes I just felt like I couldn't get it all period. But I can get it in a different you know? I could listen to a teacher and I don't know what they sayin'. Everything it's, is starting, it's just like the music everything just started fading out. I try to stay focused sometimes my mind, you know, wonders off. Just like the music, I could only listen to it for so long, especially if I'm not interested in it.

Martin's answer for this question was a little less complicated. He states,
"Plus, I mean, I'm in school. So, I'm learning everyday as far as just being in class, listening. My major right now is RTF. So, it's a lot of hands on stuff so it's not really a lot of writing."

John's learning style application experience was the most unclear. He stated,
"During high school I thought I did pretty well as a student-athlete being able to get through school. It wasn't my main, main focus, but I knew I had to pass it to get to where I wanted to get to, which was to play freshman sports. But in college it worked for a little while, but after I got into the upper level, it didn't really work as well. Then I didn't really adapt to what I really needed to do to pass."

9. *Are you in college now?*

When the participants were asked if they were still in college, one (Martin) was able to respond, "yes." Martin is still in college and is scheduled to complete his classes in the fall of 2012. Both Abraham and John are not in college now. Abraham has no immediate plan to return to college and John is planning to return to college in fall of 2012.

When Abraham was asked about not returning to college he stated, "Yeah, I'm not gonna. I think if I got back in school now, I would do way better. I think just because I got a better understanding of myself. Like I said back then the sports took me. Reality hit me. I was kinda blinded to it. Now I'm in debt."

When John was asked what motivated him to go back to college, he said, "Probably my parents cause to go to college, I mean, I know it's important."

Motivation: Inside the Mind of the African American Collegiate Football Player

10. *What do you know about the history of the male African American football college student-athlete?*

This researcher asked all of the participants if they were aware of the integration history of the male African American college football athlete. None of them were aware of it and could not say it would have definitely had an impact on how vested they were into playing football.

Martin answered, "Ummmm, probably not. If I did know the history it probably would have made me work even harder, just knowing that we had it harder. So I mean it probably would have helped if anything, a little bit."

John thought that the history may have had some influence on them if they were aware of the many struggles that were experienced by former African American college football athletes. He said, "It could have if I was coming up in that age. You know they just really had something to fight for and not just taken it as a given. It's like this is here and that's what we are supposed to play. I guess it would make a difference to know that we kind of blessed to have been able to play football."

Abraham was unaware of any history but stated that he did idolize "Deon Sanders, Jerry Rice, Steve Young, and Troy Aikman."

11. *Tell me what I would see if I walked around in your world?*

When asked what the researcher would see if she walked around in their world, each replied that they would be busy, "crazy." Martin stated that he has his hands in a lot of different things i.e. selling hair, school, and trying to be as good father. He continued, "I have a lot of things going. I have my hands dipped in a lot of different, you know. As far as three different businesses, I have my hair business, I'm going to school, and trying to be a good father. Trying to do it all."

John described his life as being up and down. He says that the researcher would see a "lot of hard work and a lot of thinking. Thinking about the next way to get that next dollar. Trying to get mo money, trying to get some money. So that I can be comfortable and have my own space."

Abraham says, "trying to build my music with my business which is "Zue Krew." We all feel like we didn't have nothing but bosses. I feel like everyone is different. You only live once, try to live it to the best of your ability. And so that's what I'm working on. That's it, working and music."

12.   If you had the opportunity to prepare for college again, what would you do differently? What would change because of it?

This was the most dynamic question asked of each of the participants. They all had a lot to say in response to this question.

Growing up, football was everything to Abraham. However, he felt football "blinded" him from life's challenges. His regrets are that he did not, "Uhh take more initiative in doing a lot of things. Getting a lot of things done from my stand point, Not depend on others to do it. I came in and let coaches handle that. My mom give me this in the dorm rooms. And I should have just taken the initiatives to do things. I should of did for myself so therefore I would know what I was doing. So when it all feel down on me, I knew from the jump. So that everything wasn't just a surprise. So that's what I would have did."

He wishes that he had more life experiences while in high school that he could have developed and transferred the skills to his college experience. These life skills would have helped him prepare for challenges that came up. He also wishes he had been allowed to work when he was in high school so that he would have had job experience when he got in college and began looking for employment.

Martin says, "I graduated with high honors, with a 3.8." His regret was not registering with the NCAA Clearinghouse while in high school. He stated, "that's what disqualified me from being eligible to play for a lot of the Division 1 colleges." Martin stated that if a student-athlete in high school wants to play football in college, he needs to make sure that business is taken care of on the athletic side as well as the academic side.

John believes that he took the easy way out and should have been more academically focused. In high school he learned how to cheat his way through school when he could. He never really studied in high school or college. As a result, he wasn't able to "adapt" to upper division academic requirements. This researcher asked John,

"So are you saying that if you had it to do again that your would have focused a little bit more on your academics? His regretfully answers, "Definitely, I definitely would have focused on my academics. I would have did so much stuff on my own and did it. And not expecting someone to bring it to me and tell me to do it. I would have been on it. I would have been like I know now. It's like, I know now you gotta be on it you can't expect someone else to do it for you. You know they will say, we cool, we cool, but no, instead of looking out for others, you gotta be able to look out for yourself."

He eventually stopped attending college due to bad grades. If he had to do it again, he would take academics learning more seriously.

The interviews were ended by asking for words of wisdom to pass on to prospective football student-athlete. They were asked to add to the topic focus, anything that would contribute to the knowledge of what would motivate the student-athlete including any roadblocks. The participants responded with the following comments:

Abraham, concerned with life skill exposure says, "Teach an athlete how to be a man. If you really gonna say he is a student-athlete, then make sure he's a student-athlete and not just an athlete. I know some friends that I got that are in the NFL, they still behind. You know?"

Martin, upset with the outcome of his preparation for being a student-athlete in college advises up and coming student-athletes, says,

"Make sure that you know what you're getting into and you know what you have to do to get there. Don't think, "I'm just gonna play football." Don't just go to school, it's a lot more. It's a lot of politics. Just know there is more to it than school and football. People get in trouble for stuff that everyday people don't even hear about. You just gotta make sure that you stay clear of all of the temptations. There is a lot of stuff I fell victim to. Be aware of what's going on. Always know people's motives, it's always motives."

John says that the, "real problems in life hit you when you stop playing football. When playing football, you don't want to "talk things into existence. "That's probably when it really needs to be talked about. And you know, punish people for not doing their school stuff. Don't let people pass. Once you get a lot people letting you pass, then you gonna run across some people that don't care about all that. They gonna give you what you deserve. That can be a hard lesson."

The interviews conducted provided sufficient information to answer all of the research questions. The learning style for this group of participants was primarily visual. It seem to predominate this group with small variations in each style.

The proposed sample size for this study was twenty (20) football athletes. Due to the seasonal timing of this study, the researcher was able to obtain a small sample group of three (3). The original choice of sample size was based on De Pablo's (2000) Probability of Missing Population Subgroup in a Random Sample Table. Such a sample would have presented a 12% risk factor for missing sub group experiences. A sample group of three (3) increases the risk factor to more than thirty-five per cent (35%). Such a large percentage means that the findings of this study cannot be used as a generalization but rather add to the body of knowledge for this focus area.

Data Analysis

The analysis for the research interviews began with transcription of field notes and audio recordings for each of the participants. Each transcript was assigned a pseudonym to assure confidentiality of the participants (Appendix 1). An inductive idiographic approach was used to discover patterns in the data that translated to emerging themes. Each line of the transcript was numbered and spaced allowed to allow for notes needed for analysis.

From the idiographic analysis notes, an initial list of themes was made for each of the participants. Because this analysis process is new to the researcher, the data collected from each of the participants was treated as if three case studies were being conducted (Appendix 2).

From the initial list of themes was completed, a cluster of themes chart was developed (Appendix 3). The cluster of themes chart was followed by the creation of a thematic codebook that would aid the research with concluding a group of emerging themes (Appendix 4).

From the theme codebook, a framework was developed for identifying final themes for this research. A chart was created for the final themes that includes the thinking process used, what was being considered, and the thinking process code assigned to each process (Appendix 5).

"Inductive analysis means that the patterns, themes, and categories of analysis come from the data; they emerge out of the data rather than being imposed on them prior to data collection and analysis" (Bowen, 2005; Patton, 1980, p. 306). Based on the framework chart, a final emerging theme chart was developed and for the purposes of reducing the chart size, only the first line of the quote to reference the theme has been included in the chart. Reference to the page and line number of each quote is provided.

Grounded theory is an example of emergence in research. An emergent methodology approach to data analysis seeks to understand the situation and discover a theory implicit in the data itself. Instead of crunching numbers to arrive at a *p* value, a grounded theory researcher uses note taking and coding to find categories or themes (akin to variables for the quantitative researcher), sorts information into meaningful patterns, and writes persuasively and creatively about whatever it is that has been discovered in the data (Bowen, 2005).

The grounded theory method was employed in my study. "A grounded theory is one that is inductively derived from the study of the phenomenon it represents. That is, it is discovered, developed, and provisionally verified through systematic data collection and analysis of data pertaining to that phenomenon" (Bowen, 2005; Strauss & Corbin, 1990, p. 23). Further, a constructivist-interpretive paradigm (Bowen, 2005; Denzin & Lincoln, 1994) underpinned my study. In line with this approach, the researcher's interpretation of data collection from the participants have provided theory construction. A constructivist-interpretive paradigm produces substantive-formal theory grounded in the research (Bowen, 2005; Denzin & Lincoln, 1994; Glaser & Strauss, 1967).

Summary of Findings

Significant amounts of data were collected during the one-on-one interviews. All participants were asked questions according to the twelve (12) question guideline. The data collected from the three student-athletes reflect a consensus on seven (7) general themes: (a) athletic identity; (b) ego identity; (c) external vs. internal motivation; (d) resilience; (e) learning styles; (f) academic identity; and (g) self-actualization.

Explanation of Themes

Athletic identity is the degree to which an individual identifies with the athlete role. All of the participants have developed some investment in sports. The two who have invested the most in football were Abraham and Martin.
Some of Abraham's statements were:
- I played football since I played Junior All American.
- I started, I'm gonna say 9, 10 years old.
- What kept me going was always to be successful. I used the football, I use my sports in my life a lot.

Martin made similar comments about being an athlete his comments included, "That was my dream, my whole life. Eat, sleep, dream, Monday through Friday, my dream, that's what I thought about all day."

John played football for a short time in his life but played an alternative sport (baseball). John played baseball most of his life. When asked how important football was he stated:
- Actually about right now it's not important at all but during that time, me playing the game, it was probably the only thing I was thinking about besides my secondary sport which was baseball.

This researcher asked, "So your sports took a good portion of your life as you were growing up?"

John responded, "Yeah, pretty much, yeah a great portion.

Interviewer: Are you playing any sports at all because I know you said you played more than one sport."

John respond, "No, I'm thinking about it but not such as now, no."

This researcher also asked, what the sport is that John is thinking about playing? His response to that question was, "Well, I was trying to look for a little baseball league. Some Sunday baseball league just to get out there. See what's good, get my swing back. Just play around, get a little in shape."

Ego Strength - develops during Erikson's ego identity stage (stage five of development. Ego strength develops with athletic identity where there is usually a conflict in role expectations for the student-athlete in middle school and high school. This is when they are forced to make priorities between school and sports. According to Asim (2006, Simiyu, 2009), while the "kids are slam dunking and flying into the end zone, they are not learning much as most colleges have confused commerce with education." The reflections the student-athletes interviewed indicated that there were some struggles with making academic choices versus athletic choices during this period as well. According to Adams (2011) to date only three empirical studies have examined this precise combination of variables (Murphy et al., 1996; Neyer, 1996; Whipple, 2009) between athletic identity and ego identity during high school.

Martin learned to make those choices during adolescence because his father would accept nothing less. He states, "My father was on my, I was no way, there was no way that I couldn't bring home nothing less than a B. During stage five (5), Martin learned that academics was more important than playing sports. He stated, "It was all about school and then it was definitely work hard in football for sure. That was probably what I would have chose. But just based on what my father, and how he was, you know, how he was. It was like, know school first and then get good grades, it would be a lot easier for you to play football and go to the school you want to go to. It was very evident by his change in demeanor of becoming more erect that Martin was just as proud of his academic status as he was his football status as he said to the researcher, "I graduated with high honors, with a 3.8." The same demeanor came up when he was asked about giving future student-athletes advice. He stated with much passion that, "School is most important. If you don't get the grades, you can't get the try out."

Martin tried to maintain a balance between his athletic and academic identities. Although the football career didn't work out, he will still be graduating from college in the year 2012. Evidence of the impact it had on ego was in his response to certain questions in his interview. Responses made that expressed his non-verbal disappointment was when three important statements were made,

1. I was really a good athlete, I was four years varsity letterman in high school, I did all that work,

2. Know what you're getting into and you know what you have to do to get there. It's a lot of politics, it's more to it than school and football. People get into trouble for stuff that everyday people don't even hear about.

3. Always know people's motives, it's always motives.

Martin's facial expressions exhibited some anger as he made these statements.

The anger was detected in his voice tone as well. His voice had a stern under tone to it and his eyes were a little a little squinted. These expressions and voice tones implied that he is still struggling with the balance of the two.

Abraham, learned to like football, first, because it was fun. He then learned to like it because it was the place where he felt he could compete with others. He stated, "My mom put me in there, I just like competing. He also stated that, "Like yeah, I compete with myself a lot. It's like a never ending."

Abraham states that he learned discipline during the adolescence period by playing football and was the only participant that revealed this information. However, because he learned to develop more athletic identity during the ego development stage, his academic identity suffered as well as his life skills development. He now struggles as to how to run his life without football. Among the statements he made was, "If football wasn't there, you know, how would I really survive? I always depended on that. And so once it was gone, I was kinda like shell shock."

External vs. Internal Motivation - explains the participants journey through his athletic involvement. External motivation being the influences on the student-athletes from family, friends, and community. Internal motivation being the influences the student-athletes have built up inside of them as a result of any innate forces or external influences. Each of them began their athletic life with parental encouragement. They all did well in sports and developed "Rock Star" mentalities in high school which transitioned through college.

Abraham's external motivation was reflected in his statement about the internal feelings he had as a result of being a football student-athlete. He stated,

"When we step into somewhere, we always standed out because we have that athletic presence. We used to, in high school, we was the man and that carried out through life." He stated, "I was the only child. Football was a reason to be around my brothers. I loved that feeling going out there and riding with my boys. I still love that to this day.

Internal motivation for Abraham appears to be on his determination to be success. It appears as if he can't be successful by being an NFL football student-athlete, he will be successful as a businessman. Abraham's ego strength includes the philosophy that hard work and his love of music will net his wealth. This is evident by his statement, "My music, Once I start that and make a mogul out of myself, I want to be more of an entrepreneur than an artist."

John reflected external motivation when he stated, "Coming up as a student athlete, you don't see, you don't see, I think we are like different people. We don't see the world like everybody else sees it. We are already stars. And are in our own, which we really be at the time because everybody knows us. Everyone expects me to do good and you do good and then you coming through and then you feel like the man.

John's internal motivation is his need to be independent. He says, "so that I can be comfortable and have my own space" and I don't want to be one of those stuck in something that I don't like doing."

Martin's external motivation appeared to be around his father. As mentioned in the ego strength stage (4.2), a good portion of his influence came from his father.

Martin's internal motivation right now is getting through school first, "It was like you know school first and then get good grades. It would be a lot easier for you. That was my motivation. A conversation about his current goals in life got the response of a list of businesses he has embarked upon. He responded:

Right now, ah, right now I have a, I'm working on having a couple of businesses. One is the hair business. And then I also plan on opening a restaurant within the next year. So I like the restaurant industry, that whole thing. I also want to get into real estate. Buying and selling you know houses and things like that, and a few other things.

Once all of the participants stopped playing football and the lime light stopped, they appeared to find something to replace the feeling they felt inside when they played sports. They honed their internal motivation to be successful took over where the external has left off. They need to accomplish goals that now come from within themselves. This also may be a defense mechanism for them because they no longer have the probability of becoming a NFL athlete. All of the participants worked hard to be successful athletes, now they are trying to meet the same level of success by working hard to meet the same level of achievement as they would have achieved in the NFL.

When all were asked about their current plans, the first response was to be either a business man.

Abraham stated that he wants to be "successful" because he wants to leave a name for himself. Both of these would have occurred had he become an NFL student-athlete. He states, "I got high expectations" and "right now I know who I am, but I'm still trying better to know what I am."

Resilience - All of the participants had tunnel vision regarding being NFL student-athletes. Once the realization set in that they will not have that opportunity, they got over it and are now trying to rewrite their future with the goal of focusing on success in their life occurring through other ventures, primarily business ventures.

While they are still trying to resolve themselves to the fact that NFL is no longer a possibility for them, they have all developed or are at least trying to develop new career plans instead of sitting around aimlessly with no plan and no motivation to develop one.

Abraham talks about his music and states that right now he is in debt and his life is pretty much, "work and music."

Martin has continued in college with the plans of graduating soon. He states he had "about a semester left." He also has a few businesses that he is trying to develop.

John has a few businesses he is trying to develop also. John states that he is trying to try being an "entrepreneur so I'm trying to get into a little bit of everything just to see what's my niche.

Both Martin and John report being in business together selling hair, making videos, and working photography.

Abraham, Martin, and John collaborate to develop music videos together.

Learning styles – Learning styles addresses how the participants learn to learn. All of the participants believe that they are visual learners. However, each have explained learning processes that include more than visual learning.

Each participant was asked how their learning styles were applied to their life.

Abraham states that he loses focus frequently. He says, "I got a way different way of learning. He was asked to explain his style and responded,

I don't know, I never been that smart I guess. My attention span is very short sometimes I just bounce around bounce around and think all day 'bout a million different things. And then like, even when I listen, I was just telling my friend, I can only listen for a while and then images start popping up in my head. So it's kind of funny, even with me with words like, I wasn't really taught how to sound to spell words out. I use my imagination and figure out how it looks. That's how I learned all of my words.

This researcher asked Abraham to explain what he meant about not being that smart. He responded by explaining his educational experience. He stated:

I never been as smart as pretty much the others in class. I was a, when I was coming up, I had resources classes. I couldn't, like other people get done with their test fast, it would mess me up, I couldn't get things, it would take me a little more time. Sometimes I just felt like I couldn't get it all, period. But I can get it in a different, you know. I could listen to a teacher, and I don't know what they sayin'. Everything it is starting, it's just like the music, everything just started fading out. I try to stay focused, sometimes my mind, you know wonders off just like the music. I could not listen to it for long, especially if I'm not interested in it.

This researcher want to know more about Abraham's wandering and asked the question, "Where does it wander off to? Abraham responded, "Whatever else I am thinking about, just anything." He also stated that with his life he is the same way, "I bounce around here and there. If I could just you know probably just slow down a little more."

Martin uses repetitive actions to include writing in order to learn. He states,

he's a "visual learner and probably a repetitive learner like the more I do it the better, obviously, the more you do it the better you get, but if I read something and then read it again and probably write it down and read it again I am able to get it as opposed to just seeing it one time. So, I think I'm a little bit of both."

While John is stating he is visual, he memorizes everything. He describes his learning style by saying that he,

"I think I'm a visual person. Listening, I might get bored and then I might think about some other stuff. But looking at it, my eyes are going to be glued to it and I'm going to remember everything I just saw that's pretty much how I learn. A lot of things by memory, remembering and seeing what I saw and then putting down the answer, that how I do stuff.

The study results of these learning styles correlate with Kunjufu's Learning Style Model (2010) which states that the three basic categories of African American learners are Visual, Oral/Auditory, and Tactile/Kinesthetic.

Academic Identity – Academic Identity is defined in this study's definition of terms, as the challenges in the educational development which includes serious stifling of achievement, aspiration, and pride in school systems. Each of the participants identified with academic identity differently. Martin has been able to balance his athletic obligations and his academic obligations so that he was able to survive in college when he dropped out of football. Abraham and John were unable to balance the two and it resulted in them dropping out of football and college. John identifies with academic identity sufficient enough to cause to him to keep trying to complete college.

On December 8, 2010, the NCAA reported releasing stunning information. The NCAA had been tracking student-athlete ethnicity for the past eleven (11) years. They have now discovered that the male African American comprises the highest percentage of football student-athletes across the nation. This phenomenon has been a first in the history of the NCAA.

According to Harper (2009), Benson (2000) found that many African American males are socialized to prioritize sports over academics when they are in high school, and the messages are sustained and amplified once they enroll in college. Academic identity also develops during the ego identity developmental stage as mentioned earlier in this report.

Self-actualization, is probably the most difficult for these participants. Located at the peak of Abraham Maslow's Hierarchy of Needs and Motivation (1943), he described this high-level need in the following way:

> "What a man *can* be, he *must* be. This need we may call self-actualization . . . It refers to the desire for self-fulfillment, namely, to the tendency for him to become actualized in what he is potentially. This tendency might be phrased as the desire to become more and more what one is, to become everything that one is capable of becoming." While the theory is generally portrayed as a fairly rigid hierarchy, Maslow noted that the order in which these needs are fulfilled does not always follow this standard progression. For example, he notes that for some individuals, the need for self-esteem is more important than the need for love. For others, the need for creative fulfillment may supersede even the most basic needs.

When reviewing Maslow's Theory of Motivation by Jen Anderson, 2011. She describes his theory as being the following:

Maslow's Theory takes the shape of a pyramid, or triangle with the most basic and pressing needs at the bottom. The five motivational needs covered in the theory, from the most basic to the most complex are: Physiological, Safety, Love/Belonging, Esteem, and Self-actualization. The bottom four layers of the pyramid contain what Maslow described as "deficiency needs" or "d-needs." These needs prompt the individual to act with the motivation of fulfilling the need when a lack is detected. With the exception of the most basic (physiological) needs, if these "deficiency needs" are not met, the body will not react, but the individual will get a feeling of restlessness. The highest need – self-actualization – can only be fulfilled once the other needs are met. This higher level need motivates an individual to seek involvement in activities that will contribute to the perfection of his or her ideal self.

For the purpose of this study, the development of self-esteem will be the focus of self-actualization. Self-esteem needs are rooted from the need to be recognized and respected by peers as well as other individuals such as the community and family. The motivation may take on different needs. It may be due to wanting to be accepted, to be noticed, or to be recognized for our achievements. Maslow presented two theories for self-esteem, the lower need and the higher need. He described the lower as the need for the respect of others, for status, recognition, fame, prestige or attention (Anderson, 2011). The higher need is for self-respect, strength, competence, mastery, self-confidence, independence, and freedom. Maslow theorizes that deprivation of these needs can lead to an inferiority complex, weakness or helplessness.

Abraham stated that he is still trying to get used to this "life thing" and finds it to be a struggle. He stated that he knows "who" he is but is not sure "what" he is. He is now working and paying off debts. He is also exploring the field of music. He says that work and music are his primary focuses right now.

Martin is probably the closest to self-actualization but he is still trying to find his way through life as well. His self-esteem appears to be more stable in that he has formed a new career plan that is coming to fruition. It is graduating from college. He proudly says, "I have about a semester to go." He has another plan in place for the next year to open up a restaurant, "I also plan on opening a restaurant within the next year.

John is going through ups and downs, which are requiring him to "think" a lot. He is searching for self but has not really discovered what self is. During his interview, this researcher, asked John what he thinks about, he stated that he was "thinking about the next way to get that next dollar, trying to get mo money. To be able to help other people that would need help."

Per Pettit (2011) coaches should build a culture that promotes self-actualized leadership, one where student-athletes progress from being directed and coached to becoming situational leaders who become passionate about their own development. The first step in the process is to give student-athletes a framework for making better decisions. Based on the interviews, these participants felt that this framework was missing from their college experience.

The overall college experience of the participants is similar. They all ended up at the same crossroads but took different journeys to get there. Abraham felt he was unprepared to be a man and be responsible which affected his ability to survive in college as a student-athlete.

Martin felt he was unprepared for the athletic career he had looked forward to all of his life because he was not groomed for the groundwork needed to take advantage of the opportunity. However, he was qualified to continue attending college because he was groomed to focus on education first and sports second.

John was used to taking short cuts in school and apparently had a rude awakening to the fact that there are no real shortcuts in life. If you take a lot of short cuts, eventually everything catches up with you. He stated that he would "cheat" off others papers or have someone give him the answers, neither worked out for him as he moved into the upper levels of college.

Below in figure 4.1 is an illustration of the emerging themes and how they are related to each other when examining learning styles relationship to motivation.

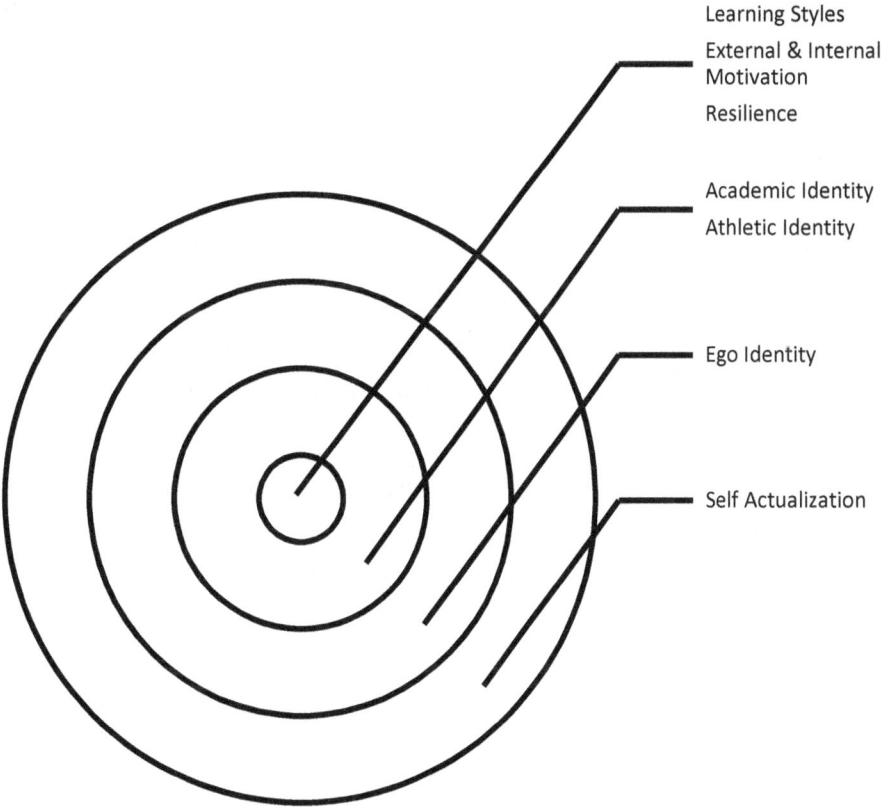

Figure 2. Self actualization is evident when ego identity is clear. Ego identity is clearer for a student-athlete when he has developed a balance between academic identity and athletic identity. Much of the outcome of this balance is based on the influences of the student-athlete's learning styles, external & internal motivation, and resilience.

Additional Results

There were additional responses that are worth mentioning that did not necessary fall into answering the guideline questions. Below are all of the responses according to each participant.

Abraham

Question: Okay and then how, what importance did it play in your life?

Answer: I didn't know. Oh, then now it's like I'm starting all of the way back from in high school. When I'm already five years out of here. Out of there because, just because of football.

Question: I always say baby steps. So, when you're looking at baby steps?

Answer: I want to be more of an entrepreneur than an artist. That's just the first step. If I can get my music out there and I can be able to change other people's situations out there, that are similar to mine. Telling my story, I end up telling someone else's story. Helping others. I always say I'll take a million people before I take a million dollars. If I got a million people in the back of me, a million dollars ain't nothing. I can get a dollar from each of them and I'll have a million dollars.

Question: My thought is an athlete should be trained to be an athlete on the field and off the field.

Answer: Yeah, on the field and off the field. And I think that is missing.

Question: Do you plan to return to college?

Answer: I definitely want to finish. I started it. That's the one thing sports taught me not to quit. That's going to be in the back of my mind regardless if I wanted it to be there or not.

Question: And you told me you were working before I put you on a tape recorder.

Answer: I work as a bartender at a hotel. Networking with people there and working on my people, working on my communication skills.

Martin

Question: Is there anything that you can add to what I've talked to you about that would help when we are looking at African American male learning styles or just that would motivate you?

Answer: You gotta make sure that you stay clear of all of the temptations there is a lot of stuff that even I fell victim to.

Question: Um um ok can you elaborate?

Answer: Just like pretty much, I was, I accepted some stuff, you know, really, as a student –athlete you not really supposed to accept certain stuff. In my case I never got in trouble for my stuff but my coach got caught for something else. It was just that because I was part of the class, I was just…..

Question: By association?

Answer: Yes, I was associated with it and so, I kinda fell victim to it.

John

Question: And what do you think was preventing you from taking advantage of it?

Answer: I'm thinking about other stuff. Trying to think about, not school pretty much, I'm thinking about the team and about how we ain't winning no games I don't even want to go to class and can't be proud about being on the team because we ain't doing nothin'. I always had to go to class and people talking about the football team and I can't just let them talk about the football team there was a lot of distractions, a lot of distractions. The ladies you know that was a distraction as well once you get in college.

Question: And so, you were having a problem really focusing on academics because everything was, the athletics was and anything relating to it was distracting? Is that what you're saying?

Answer: A lot more glamorous than books.

Question: So, I heard you say that you're going back to college what's motivating you at this point to go back to college?

Answer: To go to college I mean I know it's important but I also know that you don't need college to be successful I would like to have that paper I would like to go to college because I already, I started I might as well finish but that's that pretty much my motivation to go I know I'm going to be successful regardless I'm putting enough effort in things to just have a good back up with that it still could be an issue getting a good job and going to work. It's kind of like a rock and a hard place kind a deal, it could go anyway. It could be a waste of time either way.

Question: So now it's interesting that you mentioned that you don't have to go to college when I have been researching that has been some of the concerns of African American meant that they are thing that way. So, what makes you think that's the African American can be successful without going to college?

Answer: We are a lot more driven. Cause we, that's the kind of where, I know where our history comes from. You know the history of African American folks. We already against the odds off top. And we know that because of history, and we think to do other ways. You know the history of African American folks. We already against the odds off top. And we know that because of history, and we think to do other ways. To be working harder to get over the white man, or big head, whoever they are, African American/white or whatever the so-called man. We believe we can do that and a lot of people do. But everybody don't have it. That's just something we got from knowing our history probably. We know we can do whatever we want to do type thing.

Question: So, do you think that with all of that drive and with all of the opportunities available without having a college degree do you think those would the college degree it would be easier to open the same doors?

Answer: It could, but a lot of this day, it is about who you know, not necessary about how much you know. People can have the best of the best type or school and the best of the best type in their class. That get to that spot and they don't know the right person and who his homeboy. So, if he has the basic stuff he needs and plus he knows him, he gonna be in there. Based off of that, nine out of ten, some cases maybe not. Nine out of ten that's what is going to happen. That's what I be thinking more about me.

Question: I'd like to say is with you thinking that I guess I'm looking at trying to think about the pros and cons of what you're saying as far as having a high school diploma versus having a four year degree and being successful versus not success, so what careers do you see that can be as easily attained with a degree as without a degree,

Answer: Of course you know the given things as with sports and the music. You can invent something and start your own company, be your own boss, off the top, entrepreneurship. Anything dealing with like the longer schools, like lawyers and doctors, of course you can't just be a regular person and do that. You have to actually learn. But if you going to school to work for somebody, you can do that without going to school. You can go work for somebody without even doing that. You can go to work for old girl on the corner. If you're going to business school or something, then you be thinking about being the boss and not working under someone else.

Question: So now do you do at least research or how to be an entrepreneur and or watch videos or how are you getting your knowledge about how to be an entrepreneur?

Answer: I watched a couple of movies on a motivational speaker. Some dudes on YouTube. That's this book in there. It's called a Thousand, what's it called, a thousand entrepreneurs or a thousand bosses. It talks about all these rich men and how they got rich. How they all got rich. One thing that really took with me was that story. One of the speaker dudes that was pretty much like ah like a little Guru dude, and a regular man came and said I want to be like you. He kept saying, I want to be like you. And the Guru said meet me at the river tomorrow at 7 o'clock. So, the man said okay because I want to be like you. When he got there the Guru was in the water. So, he told the dude to step in the water, step in the water. So, the dude steps in the water and he said, get closer, closer, closer, closer, until it gets up to your neck. So. by this time he was at the guy, at the guy. So, when the dude gets a little close to him, he puts his head in the water and like he's about to drown. So, he's trying to get out the water, get out of the water. The Guru pulls his head out of the water. So, the dude ask him, why you do that? Well when you want to be successful as hard as you want to breathe right now that's successful. If you are not trying as hard as you are trying to breath than you won't ever be successful. Since I heard that I started trying to get a little more motivated that's real, that's real. You not working hard enough if you not working as if your trying to breath. That my little thing, I looked. I did research on. As far as the actual business to use the word entrepreneurship, no I haven't looked it up.

Question: Do you think that your learning styles were really addressed when you were in high school to prepare you for college or do you think that your learning styles were addressed at all while you were in college?

Answer: No cause because I don't even, I didn't even know what my learning styles were until I got to college. I would be trying to get the answers, try to cheat, looking on some else's paper, ah shoot I never, never really just studied cause to sit there and focus and just look at the words, I get bored and I just started mixing them up and thinking about a whole 'nother thing, thinking about somethin' else.

Question: How often did you utilize the counselors at school?

Answer: Not at all I went there to kick it. I didn't never go in there to use it. I didn't go in there to talk about anything.

CHAPTER FIVE: DISCUSSION

Summary of Investigation

Thousands of collegiate student-athletes are faced with the process of transition due to their athletic involvement each year. There are few systematic investigations that focus specifically on the process of transition for the collegiate athlete. Until now, researchers have primarily focused on the retirement from the professional/elite levels. As a part of the African American student-athlete's transitional process, he must learn to balance the feelings of success, fear of failure, interpersonal relationships, racism, and discrimination as they transition into adulthood.

The purpose of this study was to examine the learning styles of the male African American NCAA Division I college football student-athlete and the psychological impact it has on his motivation. By gaining more knowledge about the learning styles and motivation of the student-athlete, more effective programs can be developed to increase the African American student-athlete retention and graduation rates.

This research embarked on a journey to find answers to three questions concerning the male African American football student-athlete:

- What are the learning styles of the male African American college football athlete?
- Is there a learning style that predominates for the male African American football student-athlete?
- Does the African American football student-athlete apply his learning style to his career decision-making perception?

The data collection provided this research with information that served as an instrument to finding solutions to the learning style phenomena of the male African American student-athlete.

What are the learning styles of the male African American college football athlete?

Dr. Jawanza Kunjufu (2010) in his book, *Understanding African American Male Learning Styles*, states that, "Only twelve percent (12%) of African American boys are proficient in reading. More than seventy percent (70%) of remedial reading students are male. And lastly, seventy percent (70%) of all D's and F's are earned by males." He also states that "if you want to train students, then ask most of the questions and have pre-determined answers. If you want to educate students, however, encourage them to ask questions, and make sure the questions are open-ended."

This research found three (3) primary styles of learning for the male African American student-athlete, visual, kinesthetic, and tactile. Each of the styles require a different teaching processes in order to be effective. According to the learning styles chart of the New Hanover County Schools Instructional Services (2011), each group learns best with the following:

- Visual learning – charts, sight words, flashcards, pictures and graphics, maps, silent reading, written instructions, and computer assisted learning.
- Kinesthetic learning – playing games, role playing, reading body language, mime, drama, and learning or memorizing while moving.
- Tactile learning – learning by doing, hands-on, creating maps, building models, art projects, using manipulatives, drawing and designing, and writing and tracing.

The results of this study also found that a combination of learning styles can impact a male African American student-athlete's goal to be an elite athlete in the National Football League (NFL). The male African American student-athletic learns how to develop athletic strategies while playing football because the sport cultivates his particular learning style. The sport strengthens the student-athlete's tactile and kinesthetic skills in the football field and uses his primary visual skill to carry out the play objectives. Through feedback and creativity, he is critiqued by his coaches on his athletic style and he makes adjustments accordingly. All of the student-athlete's learning styles are employed by him while playing sports. By using his learning styles in the sport, the student-athlete is able to excel and his motivation develops to make him a star football student-athlete.

Traditionally, classroom instruction does not cultivate the male African American student-athlete in the same way. Traditional instruction for the average classroom cultivates learning styles that are counter effective for this focus group. The reality is that 21st century students are multitaskers. The findings in this research confirm that the male African American student-athlete is a multitasker. All of the participants had at least three projects going at the same time and felt as if they were moving forward on all of them. During the interviews with this researcher, they were multitasked as well (cell phones ringing, babies crying, company entering the home). It was the way they felt most comfortable.

Is there a learning style that predominates for the male African American football student-athlete?

These learning styles found in this study are representative of right-brain learners. Right-brain learners are relational learners while left-brain learners are in general, more analytical. Studies have shown that approximately two-thirds (2/3) of students in general are right brain learners. It has been found that there is an even larger percentage of African American males are visual-picture, oral/auditory, and tactile/kinesthetic learners. This information would conclude that approximately two-thirds of all male African American student-athletes are right-brain learners.

Based on research data from this study, the predominate learning style for the male African American football student-athlete is visual. Each of the participants explained their learning style as one that requires them to must see how something is working first. This would be consistent with the learning styles information presented earlier in this report.

Visual learning would also be consistent with playing the sport of football. This sport requires the student-athletes to be familiar with various plays to be executed during the game. These plays would be comparable to maps or chart. The instruction for game play is usually written to reference the play chart, again, cultivating the learning style of the student-athlete.

The kinesthetic learner and the tactile/learner styles are most related to how the participants in this study felt. After they have connected visually with an objective, they feel that they are benefiting from it. For a football student-athlete, the way he feels when he goes out on the field and executes the plays that he has learned is enormous. It also explains how he feels about the outcomes of these feelings as being terrific also.

The results of this research found that the participants expressed the same about education. They have to experience what is being taught in the classroom in order to retain the information. The data in this research found that the male African American student-athlete is very competitive and they also enjoy participating in group projects. While researching literature reviews, it was found that Kunjufu (2010) recommended cooperative learning which involves a competitive context to teaching that would maximize the academic achievement for male African Americans. Under cooperative learning, peer learning can be implemented for visual learners. Based on the data collected in this research, cooperative learning would be a good option for the student-athlete's learning process in that it would allow the student's buy in by creating a learning environment that produced similar benefits felt when the student-athlete is playing on the field.

Howard Gardener's Eight Ways of Learning

There are many models of learning styles that have been presented in educational psychology. Howard Gardener's Eight Ways of Learning (1983), Linguistic, Logical-Mathematical, Spatial, Bodily-Kinesthetic, Musical, Interpersonal, Intrapersonal, and Naturalist were found to be relative to the data collected in this research. This research found that the participants more spatial, bodily-kinesthetic, interpersonal, and musical.

A male student-athlete who is spatial thinks in images and pictures. He loves to design, draw, visualize, and doodle. In order to teach him, a teacher would need to utilize tools like art, Legos, videos, movies, imagination games, illustrated books, or maybe even trips to the museum.

A male student-athlete who is bodily-kinesthetic thinks through somatic sensations. He likes to dance, run, jump, build, touch, and gesture. He requires to learn via activities like role-playing, movement, building things, sports and physical games, tactile experiences, and hands on learning.

When interviewing Martin, he stated that his major in college was Radio, Television, and Film. He also stated that his major is primarily hands on learning at this point. He appeared to be well satisfied with his choice in education. As a football student-athlete he played the quarterback position. In this research, he has been identified as a visual bodily-kinesthetic learner. Traditionally, quarterbacks have been responsible for calling the team's offensive plays based on the defense's formation, or game situation (visual). To choose the proper play, quarterbacks often spend time rehearsing and studying prearranged plays during their team's practice sessions (bodily-kinesthetic). When Martin first began playing football, he stated he played a line position because he was "chunky" when he was younger. In football, line positions require a student-athlete to have power and endurance. You also must have knowledge of a wide variety of plays (spatial), whether they're running or passing, and be able to execute your individual responsibilities (bodily-kinesthetic). As Martin grew with age, he became less chunky and the line position was not the appropriate position for him. By coaches critiquing him and adjusting his playing style accordingly, he became a quarterback. It also compliments his spatial and bodily-kinesthetic learning styles in that they each are attracted to playing games, especially physical games.

A student-athlete which is also a musical learner thinks via rhymes and melodies. These learners love to sing, whistle, hum, tap their feet and hands, and listen. The needs for the student-athlete who is also a musical learner would include trips to concerts, playing music at home and learning to play school musical instruments.

Abraham can be identified as having spatial, bodily-kinesthetic, and musical learning styles. In his interview he discussed how he enjoys working and writing music, characteristics that were not supported in high school. His high school and college experiences included his inability to focus in class. He frequently talked about bouncing around from one thing to another. This style of learning was probably evident when he was a younger child, which is why his mother registered him in football, to teach him discipline.

Abraham might have benefited more by his mother incorporating an instrument into his learning process. This is one of the needs of musical learning styles. During conversation outside of the taped interview, it was found that Abraham is a rapper. This is appropriate for him because musical learning styles enjoy rhymes and melodies.

Abraham played the position of corner-back in football. A good corner-back understands the passing game, and the timing of receivers. He has great footwork, quickness, speed, and football instincts (About.com, Sports Football, 2012). Being a corner-back is an appropriate position for a student-athlete who is a musical learner. Such a position requires him to be rhythematic in movement and have the ability to synchronize movements of other student-athletes on the field. He was placed in a special education – resource classes because of these learning styles. Working with his learning style should have some incorporation of a music class or some style of rhythematic expression as a way of learning difficult subjects. Surprisingly, this position also requires the student-athlete to have the ability to focus on one student-athlete because they are often assigned "man-to-man coverage." He reports being successful on the football field at being focused but not in the classroom. While Abraham is reporting a problem with focusing on daily life skills as well as his music development, this research found that it is possibly due to the lack of connection during his stage 5 psychosocial development. This conclusion is based on his comment that he feels he has returned to "high school" as he is learning life skills during this phase of his life.

The last way of learning from Gardener's (1983) list of eight ways that is applicable to these participants is interpersonal learning. Interpersonal learners like to bounce ideas off other people. They love to be leaders, organize, relate, manipulate, mediate, and party. They learn well through having friends, group games, social gatherings, community events, clubs, mentors, and apprenticeships.

Results of this research found that all of the participants in this research appear to be interpersonal learners. However, John appears to match the process most. During John's discussion about his college experience, the most damaging event affecting his motivation was other college students talking about the football team. He found himself frustrated with the constant comments about the team's lack of wins. John found himself always defending the team in class because he "couldn't let them talk about the team." John's learning style most fits Gardener's (1983) spatial, bodily-kinesthetic, interpersonal categories.

John has the least definitive learning style in that his interview implied that he depended on the actions of his fellow classmates to get him through school. He admits that he often "cheated on tests" or would get the information from another source versus studying. A more effective way of John using his interpersonal style of learning would include finding friends who were willing to accommodate John's learning style. John would have benefitted from study groups. There he would feel as if he was experiencing learning with other people in a non-structured environment.

John used his interpersonal relationships with students was more difficult as he went through college because answers became more difficult to find. Upper level classes often require the learner to be creative. It's hard to copy someone's creativity. Upper level classes require the student-athlete to study, something that John has admitted that he has never done. He stated,

> I didn't even know what my learning styles were until I got to college. I would be trying to get answers, try to cheat, looking on some else's paper. Shoot, I never, never, really just studied, cause to sit there and focus and just look at the words, I get bored and I just started mixing them up and thinking about a whole 'nother thing. Thinking about somethin' else.

John was assigned the position of offensive line backer. This is a position that requires size, strength, speed, and intelligence. The offensive lineman's size is important because the game of football requires them to use their momentum (bodily-kinesthetic) to drive defense student-athletes away from the line of scrimmage. The team (interpersonal) relies on the lineman's strength to gain an advantage on every play. Offensive linemen use their speed to block student-athletes on outside running plays, and for blocking beyond the line of scrimmage. They must also study the tendencies of the opposition (spatial), so they can gain a split-second advantage when the ball is snapped. In summary, the position of offensive line backer is one of the most physical positions in the game. Because John's learning style is not as clear as the other two participants, this study believes that he may still be taking short cuts by mimicking other's learning style. This conclusion is based on the fact that John did not explain his learning style with the same level of non-verbal conviction and clarity that the other participants had. He reports that he was not aware of his learning style until he was in college and was never tested or counseled. The conclusion would be that he learned from interpersonal conversations with peers. In order for John to have a clear understanding of his learning style, this research finds that it would be wise for him to pursue basic career development testing through his school counselor.

Does the male African American college football student-athlete apply his learning style to his career decision-making perception?

The results of this study found that the perception of the male African American football student-athlete is affected by his learning style. His learning style relies more on what he can see, touch, and make happen. Academically, he would have to see the results of acquiring education as an independent outcome, separate from sports. The average African American student-athlete learns to see the relationship between education and sports as a means to an end. The means is to make decent grades in high school so that he can end up playing football in college.

The new message for the football student-athlete should be, good grades need to be earned to get in college and then maintained in order to stay in college, if they want to play football. The student-athlete does not focus on the consequences of not maintaining good grades in college, no college football. John, "You not really thinking that, that's gonna happen, if you do or if you don't, you can't be talking things into existence."

African American male football student-athletes who are visual learners may benefit well from having mentors (possibly ex-athletes) that are able to help them visualize the connection between being an elite athlete and an elite college student as well. According to Harrison (2010), African American student-athletes need encouragement to begin their preparation for life after sports. According to Sack & Staurowsky (1998):

> Cut off from other avenues for social mobility and inspired by a pantheon of African American athletic heroes, many young African Americans have dedicated their early lives to sports. It is from this talented pool of highly motivated African American athletes that the college sport industry has increasingly drawn its athletic labor. Providing academic opportunities for minorities has had little to do with this pattern of recruitment (pp. 104 – 105).

While modeling was not discussed during this research, the participant, Martin, talked about his father stressing the importance of obtaining good grades in school and how it was a priority in his home. He appeared to follow the convictions of his father which has resulted in him having a better learning experience in college. He is also the one who has continued to apply his learning style to his life as he is maturing by reading, writing, and then reading again for clarity and understanding. Martin stated that he needed to see what he was learning followed by writing it down, then looking at the learning objective again. Martin has been able to transfer his learning style to organizing his lifestyle by developing the ability to make a daily agenda of what his day should look like. Martin: "If I read something and then read it again and probably write it down and read it again, I am able to get it as opposed to just seeing it one time."

John stated that he needed to see the learning objective afterwards he would memorize the objective. If John was unable to visualize the objective, he would look to one of his peers for the answer. When interviewing John, it doesn't appear as if he has been successful applying his learning style to his career decision-making. He admits that he has only considered his learning style since he has been in college. It is in college that he discovered that his style was ineffective for higher learning. Based on the findings in this research, John would benefit well from a mentor.

Learning Disabilities

An additional finding in this research is the possible existence of untreated learning disabilities that may affect the motivation of a student-athlete. Abraham stated that he not only had to see the learning objective but he also had to relate to it. If he was unable to relate to the object he would get bored. Abraham also expressed that he had an inability to focus for a length of time. He often finds himself losing focus and bounce around from one thing to another. When discussing with Abraham how he has applied his learning style to his career decision making, he expressed that he is still having the same problems in life, staying focused. There are indicators from his interview that Abraham's learning style may include a learning disability such as ADHD. During the interview he discussed his educational history included having "resource classes" in high school. Further discussion did not include a diagnosis or whether he was provided extra resources for learning in college.

According to the Mayo Clinic (2011), there is a difference between a normal child and a child with ADHD. According to the Mayo Clinic the differences are that,

> "Most healthy children are inattentive, hyperactive or impulsive at one time or another. It's normal for preschoolers to have short attention spans and be unable to stick with one activity for long. Even in older children and adolescents, attention span often depends on the level of interest. Most teenagers can listen to music or talk to their friends for hours but may be a lot less focused about homework.
>
> The same is true of hyperactivity. Young children are naturally energetic — they often wear their parents out long before they're tired. And they may become even more active when they're tired, hungry, anxious or in a new environment. Some children naturally have a higher activity level than do others. Children should never be classified as having ADHD just because they're different from their friends or siblings."

Without a follow up interview with Abraham, it would be unfair to conclude that he suffers from ADD/ADHD. On the surface, it would appear that he does suffer from ADD/ADHD based on the findings in this research. The findings also reveal that he now suffers from adult ADD/ADHD that is untreated.

Mayo Clinic (2012) describes normal behavior versus ADHD behavior as,

> "Some people having personalities with certain characteristics common that are with ADHD. The clinic states that ADHD is diagnosed only when symptoms are severe enough to cause ongoing problems in multiple areas of one's life. In adults with ADHD, these persistent and disruptive symptoms can be traced back to early childhood."

Diagnosis of ADHD in adults can be difficult because certain ADHD symptoms are similar to those caused by other conditions, such as anxiety or mood disorders. To make it even more challenging, half of the adults who have ADHD also have at least one other diagnosable mental health condition, such as depression or anxiety (Mayo Clinic, 2012).

This research found that Abraham may have suffered from ADHD as a child and while it may have been addressed in childhood and adolescence, when he transitioned to college, he did not address this learning disability, and has not addressed it in adulthood. According to Morgan (2012), "students with ADHD do not adequately plan their college transitions, relied heavily on family for assistance with their transition and medical treatment, did not utilize many campus resources available to them, and lacked strategies to manage their ADHD symptoms." Research by Carlson & Mann (2002), suggests that students with ADHD learn well when they are highly interested and show improved behavior or academic performance when tasks are made more salient, novel, or interesting. When Abraham was asked what he would do differently when preparing for college, he responded, "I would take more initiative in doing a lot of things. Getting a lot of things done from my standpoint. Not depend on others to do it. I came in and let coaches handle that, my mom give me this in the dorm rooms, and I should have just taken the initiatives to do things. I should have did for myself so therefore I would know what I was doing."

Emerging Themes

In chapter four, seven (7) general themes were presented as being found in this research, a) Athletic Identity; b) Ego Identity; c) External vs. Internal Motivation; d) Resilience; e) Learning Styles; f) Academic Identity; g) Self-Actualization. Each of these play an important part in the development of a male African American student-athlete's complex development.

Based on previous literature and the utilization of multiple theoretical frameworks, this research found that these general themes are salient when examining the learning styles and motivation of the male African American football student-athlete.

Erickson's Psychosocial Theory

Erickson's stage five (5) of his psychosocial theory refers to the adolescent stage of growth in human development. This is also the stage when, most males first become active in sports and their level of talent in the sport is exposed (ages 12 to 18 years). According to Erickson's theory, teens need to develop a sense of self and personal identity. Success leads to an ability to stay true to oneself, while failure leads to role confusion and a weak sense of self. Each of the participants in this study expressed some struggle with developing a sense of self in that they are now finding themselves having to redefine who they are. They are no longer playing football (which was always part of their identity) and must learn how to exist in a world where football is not the primary focus in life.

Academic, Athletic, and Ego Identity are significant phases of development during stage five of Erickson's theory. All three identities contribute to the strength of the ego. The ego will develop either way but the strength of its direction is based on the strength of support received from academics and athletics external and internal motivators.

This study found that the life experiences of the student-athlete as he passes through stage five (5) has a great effect on how he learns how to learn. Based on literary research presented earlier, his exposure to the appropriate type of teacher and other external motivators will help determine the strength of his internal motivation and his ability to be resilient (Harrison, 2010). The three must work together like a well-oiled machine in order to produce a well-developed student-athlete as shown in figure 4.2.

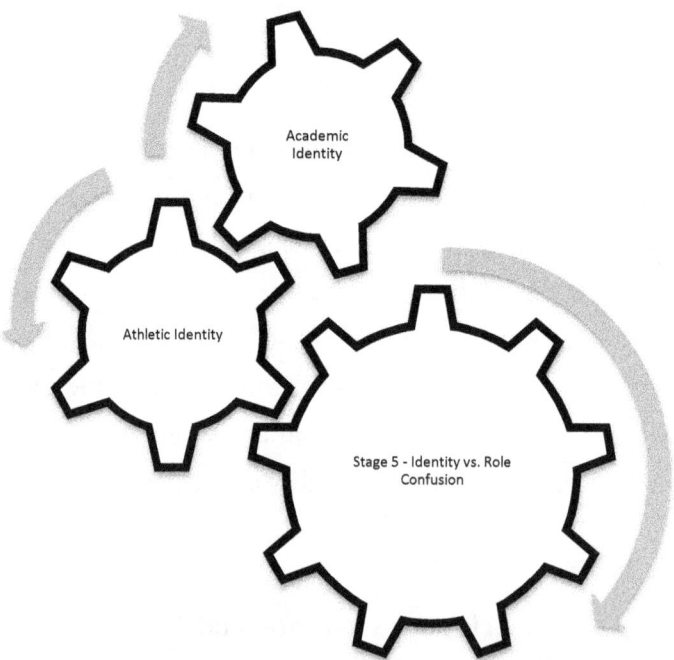

Figure 3. As Stage 5, Identity vs. Role Confusion, is moving forward, the strength of either Athletic Identity or Academic Identity will determine its direction.

It is the learning styles that the student-athlete learns during stage five (5) that he takes with him to college (Morgan, 2012). In order for him to be strong enough to survive the bigger challenges in college, he must have developed the skills and the tools necessary for the task of focusing on both while in high school.

Abraham and John appear to have struggled with academics in high school and learned how to get by. Abraham became a part of the special educational system which gave him more exposure special educators who were teaching, not necessarily according to his learning style. This would have caused him to spend his adolescent development period in special education classes also known as resource classes. Per Abraham, "I loved going out there competing and strapping up." Academically he did not feel the same level of competition. Academically he learned to feel inferior and different and stated, "I don't know, I never been that smart, I guess. My attention span is very short, sometimes I just bounce around." While Abraham did not say it, his non-verbal expressions are that he still does not believe he is smart. This is the attitude he took to college with him. Academically he was deficient but athletically he was excellent. Now that he is no longer playing football, he finds himself looking for answers that he should have started to find in high school, "I didn't know, now it's like I'm starting all of the way back from high school, when I'm already five years out of there. Out of there, just because, just because of football."

John appears to have passed through adolescence through shortcuts. He appears to have the foundation to have a somewhat balance athletic and academic identity. This is based on his statement that he knew he had to make good grades to "play freshman ball" in college. John transferred his learning styles of taking shortcuts to college and found it ineffective as he got to the "upper level classes." He believes that his learning style is still visual. He has plans to attend college in the fall. He would benefit well by actively engaging with the counseling and academic supports on campus to re-direct him on how to apply his learning styles appropriately. During his interview, John stated that his biggest problem in college was "adapting" his learning style to the information provided in class.

Additional Findings

Additional findings during this research found that all participants have experienced difficulty transitioning from pedagogy to andragogy which this researcher has name Andragogy Transformation. Andragogy Transformation for the student-athlete occurs when he has developed athletic identity during Erickson's psychosocial stage five, identity vs role confusion and transfers this same mentality to college from high school. Andragogy Transformation is a combination of adolescence and extended adolescence (Gordon-Nichols, 2012). Adolescence occurs during the ages of 11 to eighteen 18 years (Erickson, 1950) and extended adolescence occurs between the ages of 18 years and 25 years (Arnett, 2004; See figure 4.3).

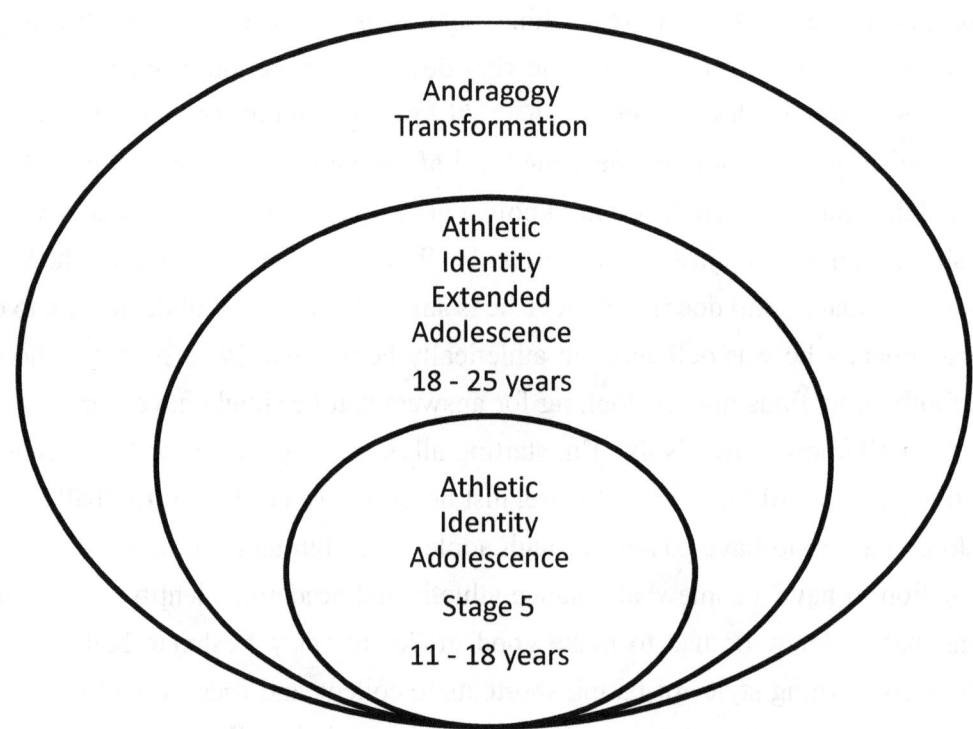

Figure 4.3.

Andragogy Transformation is the period of child/adult development between the ages of 11 years to 25 years when self-identity is formed.

Contributions of Findings

Earlier literature reviews for this research found that the relationship between the learning styles of the male African American and their motivation can be based on the Experiential Learning Theory (ELT) by David A. Kolb (1984) as presented in Chapter One, page 13.

Additional information presented included Dr. Jawanza Kunjufu (2010) in Chapter One, page 13, who stated that the male African American should be taught according to his learning style preference in order to enhance his success rate in higher education.

The findings for this study were that Dr. Kunjufu's LSM (2010) and Dr. Kolb's ELT (1984) were the models that were most in alignment with the learning styles/motivation relationship of the student-athletes that participated in this study.

A psychosocial exploration was conducted to determine if the learning styles of a male African American student-athlete has a psychological impact on his motivation. Erickson's psychosocial stage development model, addresses ego development, and was found to be the most identifiable explanation for the relationship.

One of the main elements of Erikson's psychosocial stage theory is the development of ego identity. Ego identity is the conscious sense of self that we develop through social interaction. According to Erikson, our ego identity is constantly changing due to new experiences and information we acquire in our daily interactions with others. Each stage in Erikson's theory is concerned with becoming competent in an area of life. If the stage is handled well, the person will feel a sense of mastery, which is sometimes referred to as ego strength or ego quality. If the stage is managed poorly, the person will emerge with a sense of inadequacy (Cherry, 2012). The results of the data from this research is that the participants are currently feeling a somewhat inadequate and all are trying to remold themselves in order to feel good about themselves again.

A student-athlete's learning styles should be incorporated with his ego strength by the time he reaches college. The intensity of his ego strength will also affect his motivation. The direction his ego strength is moving as he transitions through life will impact his ability to be successful. Erickson's Identity vs Role Confusion developmental stage is when ego and athletic identity begin to develop. The student-athlete should be learning how to balance athletic identity and academic identity during this time period. As the student-athlete in this study begin to re-shape their future, they must continue to reassess their learning style using andragogy learning methods versus pedagogy methods in order to make an effective transformation to an ego strength that is less dependent on a sports mentality.

The results of this study found that the psychological impact of a male African American college student-athlete's learning styles on his motivation to be a considerable finding. This study found that it is the learning style and ego strength that determines the impact of motivation for the student-athlete. It is the combination of learning style, ego strength, and motivation that impact how the student-athlete is able to achieve andragogy transformation. Andragogy transformation (Gordon-Nichols, 2012) begins during the adolescent stage of development (ages 11–18 years) and should end during the extended stage of adolescent development, (ages 18–25 years). For the purpose of learning styles, a student-athlete should transition out of the teacher having the full responsibility for making decisions about what will be learned (pedagogy) to the student-athlete taking the initiative to decide what will he will learn (andragogy) during andragogy transformation. Theoretically, when the male African American student-athlete masters andragogy transformation, he will be observed as exhibiting mostly adult behaviors and characteristics.

Andragogy Learning

In 1984, Malcolm Knowles, introduced an andragogy theory which attempted to specifically address adult learning. Knowles (1984) emphasizes that adults are self-directed and expect to take responsibility for decisions. Based on Knowles theory, it is important that student-athletes develop a learning style that compliments andragogy learning versus pedagogy learning. If he is able to accomplish this, he will have developed learning styles that reflect andragogy learning. His motivation will also transform from adolescent values and ideas to adult values and ideas.

This study has shown that the learning style of the student-athlete can directly affect his motivation. This is based on the outcome of his psychosocial development. It is during the andragogy transformation phase that the student-athlete learns self-awareness and self-actualization about his sport and academic ranking. He should be able to assess his ranking and develop his career path accordingly. If a student-athlete is able to transition from pedagogy to andragogy, he most likely will be able to not only have motivation but also have developed a good balance between his academic and athletic commitments.

After interviewing all of the participants, this researcher found that all were at different stages of the andragogy transformation. Abraham appears to be at the beginning stages of late adolescence evidence by him stating that he is behind in growing up and is learning things that he should have learned in high school.

John appears to be in the middle stages of the andragogy transformation in that he states that he still be exploring what adult expectations feel comfortable for him. John is still trying to find balance between athletic identity and academic identity in that he still wants to play recreational baseball and still wants to go to college and receive his degree to use as a "back up" plan for his future.

Martin appears to have just about completed his transformation in that he was more concise when expressing his goals and ambitions. He has learned to balance athletics and academics and recommends education as a primary focus for student-athletes.

There have been ongoing debates regarding intercollegiate athletics and whether they negatively affect the psychosocial development (Blann, 1985; Sowa & Gressard, 1983) of student-athletes. Another question that should be pondered is: "Does intercollegiate athletic participation support the psychological development of the male African American college football athletes?" This question would be especially important when it relates to Division 1 colleges where athletic identity can easily outweigh academic identity.

According to the (Hosik 2011) findings from the student-athlete 2010-2011 study show a second consecutive year of male African American student-athletes constituting most of the participants in Division I football.

As of 2011, 61% of the African American student-athletes graduated from college in six years from entry (NCAA, 2011). This isolated report of success is impressive, however when compared to White male football student-athletes, it paints a different picture. When compared to White male football student-athletes, there is an 80% graduation rate from college. When the comparison is made between African American football student-athletes and their cohorts, White football student-athletes, the graduation rate is disproportioned.

Research involving the relationship between a male African American student-athlete's learning style and his motivation continues to be limited empirically. This study will provide information that should lend to the bank of information available to counselors, teachers, psychologists, and administrators who work with student-athletes both directly and indirectly. It is anticipated that knowledge contributed from this study will cause them to implement more effective interventions. This study should provide an avenue of communication between student-athletes and counselors that will provide better access to opportunities that encourages them to seek out university and athletic personnel for personal resolutions that affect their athletic, academic, and lifelong careers.

As this study adds to the literature regarding male African American student-athletes motivation. It has been found that motivation determines whether the student-athlete completes college. As the male African American student-athlete increases in number at predominately white colleges, the understanding of their motivational development issues is important (Helms, 1990; McEwen & Roper, 1994). Cross-cultural competencies for coaches, administrators, faculty and staff become very essential to andragogy transformation. Cross-cultural competencies must address the psychosocial and learning style development of the male African American football student-athlete in order to improve the current systems. Researchers have said that the athletic environment plays a vital role in facilitating psychosocial developmental of student-athletes (Chickering & Reisser, 1993).

By addressing the relationship between the African American football student-athlete's learning style and motivation, intervention strategies, career development programs, and counseling and advisement programs can be implemented. The long-term outcome should be more African American student-athletes graduating from college.

Theory Implications

As discussed in the research, Cross (1971) suggested that African Americans transition through different stages of racial consciousness characterized by denial of their African Americanness to a stage characterized by acceptance of their African Americanness. He also suggested that African Americans encounter more barriers to racial identity development than Whites. This theory, when applied to the male African American football student-athlete, may serve as a subconscious influence in the student-athlete's psychosocial development.

The complex experience of the student-athlete transitioning his high school football imaginings to college football imaginings creates a superficial impression of his future lifestyle. If he buys into this impression, athletic identity will over power academic identity, resulting in his ego strength visions being directed toward an athletic future.

As define earlier, athletic identity is the degree to which an individual identifies with the athlete role. Once athletic identity begins to overpower the student-athlete, it creates identity foreclosure. When identity foreclosure sets in, andragogy transformation is decelerated. Deceleration of andragogy transformation will lower the male African American's motivation to develop a career plan outside of playing football in the NFL.

Practice Implications

Implications from this research contribute to the profession of counselor education and counseling by providing information about how the male African American college football student-athlete's learning style impacts his motivation. It also provides more affirmative information on the root to his motivation. By acknowledging the relationship of the student-athlete's learning style and the ability to transform into adulthood, successful interventions can be developed by counselors and educators that concurrently addresses the two issues.

Training classes should include a program of study that increases the understanding of both cross-cultural counseling and cross-cultural education concepts that incorporate the psychology of social and educational development. By using this approach, more attention can be focused on the holistic development of the male African American college football student-athletes' skill development.

Counseling services are underutilized by male African American student-athletes as a whole as were reported by one of the participants. The results of this study imply that a more proactive effort should be incorporated in the implementation of student-athletes program development for the male African American football student-athletes.

Proactive effort to implement football student-athletic development programs should begin while the athlete is in middle-school or high school as part of the school curriculum. This would involve developing an educational track for athletes that address the challenges that typically arise when one becomes an elite athlete. This track would include reading, writing, and arithmetic being to taught to football student-athletes as it relates to what their life would look like if they were in the NFL.

For counseling services to be beneficial to student-athletes, a strategy enhancement including housing a counselor in the same building with the coaches would be beneficial. This enhancement strategy should include coaches concurrently becoming involved with and collaborating with the school/college counselor in the education process of the football student-athlete as they are in the athletic process. An ongoing evaluation of student support services aimed at assessing student satisfaction and student outcomes (GPA, grades, overall progress) is critical to the success of increasing the motivation of football student-athlete outside of the sport of football.

Limitations

This was a small sample and generalization for such a complex group of individuals would require more time to locate and coordinate a larger group of participants.

Recommendations for Future Research

This study was solely based on qualitative data collection to determine the need for future qualitative studies. The results of this study would warrant consideration of being researched as a mixed method project to include the Myers Briggs personality test and an emotional intelligence test as a factor into the student-athlete's motivation. By conducting a mixed method research project, the information will provide a more intensive and detailed outcome for this subject matter.

Additional suggested research projects are:
- What is the psychological impact on motivation by teaching life skills classes to the male African American college football student-athlete during his freshman year in college?

- This study examined Division I colleges only. Lower NCAA divisions require more lenient academic requirements to enroll in their college. The level of competition, budget, and size of school also differs. A study should be conducted to determine how the learning style of a male African American football student-athlete in a Division II and Division III colleges psychologically impacts motivation. The goal would be to determine if the findings are changed.

- A recommended study is the relationship of the assigned football playing position for the male African American student-athlete on his ability to complete andragogy transformation.

- This study is a small contribution to the pool of knowledge available. Additional qualitative research is needed to investigate other issues that serve as barriers for the male AA college football student-athlete's psychosocial development. The more intensive the studies conducted are, the greater the anticipation that myths and stereotypes will decrease.

Summary

The gaps in literature are decreasing as the interest in intercollegiate athletic participation continue to become more significant on the overall impact of college sports. The male African American student-athlete has now moved to the top of the "food chain" in respect to football ethnic representation in the NCAA football programs. This change in position has caused the African American student-athlete to now become visible in ways that were never considered before. The voice of learned helplessness was once only a whisper. Now it speaks volumes to problems that had been rising over the years.

The educational system continues to fail our male African American football student-athletes by being resistant to change and not developing programs that are perfect for high-energy, right-brained learners. This researcher posits this is the same high-energy that has benefited revenue earning colleges since the full integration of football in 1972.

The NCAA now hears the voices of complaints that have coined the phrase of the "miseducation of the Negro" existing in our higher educational system loud and clearly. The NCAA has now implemented programs to correct a grievous error overlooked for the sake of the football programs by adopting a comprehensive academic reform package designed to improve the academic success and graduation of all student-athletes. Colleges are now being penalized for not executing programs that increase the Graduation Success Rate (GSR) of their student-athletes and being rewarded for their successes. As of December, 2011, the NCAA is considering increasing the required Grade Point Averages (GPA) that makes student-athletes eligible to play sports.

For Historically Black Colleges and Universities, NCAA has committed to helping them with program development that improves the academic performance of their male African American football student-athletes.

The hope is that as the eligibility guidelines change, learning style accommodations for teaching the male African American football student-athlete will also shift future football student-athletes psychosocial development more towards academics. The results of this shift in the psychosocial development of the male African American football student-athlete will increase their motivation and it will affect college retention and the graduation success rate should increase.

REFERENCES

Adams v. Richardson, 480 F2d 1159 (D.C. Cir 1973).

Adams, J. C. (2011). *Athletic identity and ego identity status as predictors of career maturity among high school students.* ProQuest Dissertations and Theses, 2011. htpp://udini.proquest.com/view/athletic-identity-and-ego-identity-pqid:2408751901/.

Anderson, J. (2011). *Maslow Theory of Motivation.* Retrieved from www.selfdevelopment.net/motivation/motivation-basics/maslow-theory-of-motivation.

Arnett, J. J. (2004). *Emerging adulthood: The winding road from the late teens through the twenties.* New York, NY: Oxford University Press.

Asim, J. (2006). Book review. *The crisis.* November/December, 48-49.

Banks, A. (2005). *The effects of a psychoeducational life skills class on the psychosocial development of student-athletes.* (unpublished doctoral dissertation). Texas Tech University. Texas Tech University Library | Mail Stop 40002 | Lubbock, TX 79409-0002

Bell, D. (1992b). *Race, racism, and American law*. Boston, MA: Little, Brown.

Blann, W. F. (1985). Intercollegiate athletic competition and students educational and career Plans. *Journal of College Student Personnel, 26,* 115-118.

Blumer, H. (1954). What is wrong with social theory? *American Sociological Review, 18*, 3-10.

Bowen, G. A. (2005). *Service learning in higher education: Giving life and depth to teaching and learning* [Booklet No. 7]. Cullowhee, NC: Coulter Faculty Center, Western Carolina University.

Bowles, T. (2004). *Adult approaches to learning and associated talents*. Australian Journal of Educational and Developmental Psychology, 4, 1-12.

Boykin, W. (1983). *On task performance and Afro-American children.* In U. R. Spencer (Ed.), *Achievement and Achievement Motives* (pp. 324-371). Boston, MA: W. H. Freeman & Co.

Brooks, I. (2009). *Organizational behaviour: Individuals, groups, and organizations.* (4th Ed. Illustrated). ISBN: 0273715364. Prentice Hall/Financial Times. Pearson Education Ltd. United Kingdom.

Carlson C. L., & Mann M. (2002). Sluggish cognitive tempo predicts a different pattern of impairment in the attention deficit hyperactivity disorder, predominantly inattentive type. *Journal of Clinical Child and Adolescent Psychology, 31*(1), 123-129. PMID 11845633.

Cassara, J. (2011). *College football's gentleman's agreement, the history of the sports unofficial policy of racial exclusion.* Retrieved from http://johncassara.net/history.html

Cherry, K. (2012). *Erickson's Theory of Psychosocial Development*. About.com Guide. Retrieved from http://psychology.about.com/od/psychosocialtheories/a/psychosocial.htm

Chickering, A. W., & Reisser, L. (1993). *Education and identity.* San Francisco, CA: Jossey-Bass.

Cross, W. E. (1971). The Negro-to-African American conversion experience: Towards a psychology of African American liberation. *African American World, 20*, 13-27.

Denzin, N. K. & Lincoln, Y. S. (1994). *Introduction: Entering the field of qualitative research.* In N. K. Denzin & Y. S. Lincoln. (Eds. p. 361). Handbook of qualitative research. Thousand Oaks, CA: Sage.

DePaulo, P. (2000). *Sample size for qualitative research.* Quirks Marketing Research Review. Retrieved from http://www.quirks.com/articles/a2000/20001202.aspx?searchID=241862844

Donner, J. K. (2005). Towards an interest-convergence in the education of African American football student-athletes in major college sports. *Race ethnicity and education, 8*(1), 45-67. Retrieved from http://wm.academia.edu/JamelDonnor/Papers/448355/Towards_An_Interest-Convergence_In_the_Education_of_African_American_Football_Student_Athletes_In_Major_College_Sports

Edelin, R. (1995). The infusion of African and African American content: A question of content and intent. In Hilliard, A., Payton-Stewart, L. & Williams, L. (Eds.), *Infusion of African and African American content in the school curriculum.* (2nd Ed. p. 7). Chicago, IL: Third World Press.

Edwards, H. (1984). The African American 'dumb jock:' An American sports tragedy. *College Board Review, 131*, 8–13.

Erikson, E. H. (1968). *Identity: youth and crisis.* New York, NY: W. W. Norton & Company, Inc.

Farmer, E. (2011). *Colleges fight to get and keep African American males.* Retrieved from wiretapmag.org/education/44665/

Ferguson, T. (2009). Combating unseen struggles: The African American male football student-athlete. *Journal of the Indiana University Student Personnel Association.* 2009 Edition.

French, S. E., Seidman, E., Allen, L., & Albert, J. L. A. (2006). The development of ethnic identity during adolescence. *Developmental Psychology, 42*(1), 1-10.

Gardner, H. (1983). *Frames of mind: The theory of multiple intelligences.* New York, NY: Basic Books.

Gardner, H. (1993). *Frames of mind* (Revised Ed.). New York, NY: Basic Books.

Gardner, H. (1999). *Intelligence reframed.* New York, NY: Basic Books.

Gardner, H. (2003). *Intelligence in seven Steps.* New Horizons for Learning, Creating the Future. http://www.newhorizons.org/future/CreatingtheFuture/crfut_gardner.html

Glaser, B. G., & Strauss, A. L. (1967). *The discovery of ground theory: Strategies for qualitative research.* Chicago, IL: Aldine.

Hale, J. (2001). *Learning while Black: Creating educational excellence for African American children.* Baltimore, MD: The Johns Hopkins University Press.

Harper, S. R. (2009). *Race, interest convergence, and transfer outcomes for African American male student-athletes.* http://works.bepress.com/cgi/viewcontent.cgi?article=1028&context=sharper.

Harrison, K. C., & Lawrence, S. M.. (2010). *African American student-athletes' perceptions of career transition in sport: A qualitative and visual elicitation.* Philadelphia, PA: Routledge.

Helms, J. E. (1990). *African American and White racial identity: Theory, research, and practice.* New York, NY: Greenwood Press.

Hosick, M. B. (2011). *NCAA working with HBCUs to clear APR barriers.* National Collegiate Athletic Association. Retrieved from http://NCAA.org.

Jackson-Allen, J., & Christenberry, N. (1994). *Learning style preferences of low- and high-achieving young African-American males.* Paper presented at the Annual meeting of the Mid-South Educational Research Association, Nashville, TN.

Kemper, K. E. (2004). The smell of roses and the color of student-athletes: College football and the expansion of the civil rights movement in the West. *Journal of Sport History, 31*(3), 33.

Knowles, M. (1984). *The adult learner: A neglected species.* Houston, TX: Gulf Publishing.

Kolb, D. A. (1984). *Experiential learning.* Englewood Cliffs, NJ: Prentice Hall.

Kunjufu, J. (2011). *Understanding black male learning styles.* African American Images. Chicago, IL.

Lewis, J. (2012). *How to play cornerback.* Retrieved from http://football.about.com/od/howtoplaycoach/a/How_to_Play_Cornerback.htm

Lundy, G. (2003). School resistance in American high schools: The role of race and gender in oppositional culture theory. *Evaluation and Research in Education, 17*, 6-24.

Mayo Clinic Staff. (2011). *Attention-deficite/hyperactivity-disorder (ADHD) in children.* Retrieved from http://www.mayoclinic.com/health/adhd/DS00275

McDougal, S. (2009). "Break it down:" One of the cultural and stylist instructional preferences of African American males. *The Journal of Negro Education, 78*(4), 432-440.

McEwen, M. K.. & Roper, L. D. (1994). Incorporating multiculturalism into student affairs preparation programs: Suggestions from the literature. *Journal of College Student Development, 35*, 46-53.

McEwen, M. K., Roper, L. D., Bryant, D. R., & Langa, M. J. (1990). Incorporating the development of African American students into psychosocial theories of student development. *Journal of College Student Development, 31,* 429-436.

Melandez, M. C. (2008). African American football student-athletes on a predominantly White college campus: Psychosocial and emotional realities of the African American college athlete experience. *Journal of African American Psychology, 34*(4), 423-451.

Morgan, K. (2012). *The college transition experience of students with ADHD [Abstract].* An Abstract Dissertation, Doctor of Philosophy. Kansas State University, Manhattan, Kansas. Retrieved from http://hdl.handle.net/2097/13741.

Murphy, G. M., Petitpas, A., & Brewer, B. W. (1996). Identity foreclosure athletic identity and career maturity in intercollegiate athletics. *The Sport Psychologist, 10,* 239-246.

National Collegiate Athletic Association (NCAA). (2011). *African Americans gain first majority in Division I football.* NCAA Media Center. Retrieved from http://www.ncaa.org/wps/wcm/connect/public/ncaa/resources/stats/football/index.html

Neyer, M. (1996). *Identity development and career maturity patterns of elite resident athletes at the United States Olympic Training Center* (Unpublished doctoral dissertation). University of Florida, George A. Smathers Libraries, Gainsville, Florida,

Orchard, T. (2011). *Mental performance reaction to game momentum change.* Student Athletic Recruitment Services. Retrieved from http://noblesteps.com/blog/.

Orlikowski, W. J., & Baroudi, J. J. (1991). Studying information technology in organizations: Research approaches and assumptions. *Information Systems Research.*

Parham, W. (1993). The intercollegiate athletes: A 1990s profile. *The Counseling Psychologist, 21*, 411-428.

Patton, M. Q. (2002). *Qualitative research & evaluation methods* (3rd Ed.). Thousand Oaks, CA: Sage Publications.

Patton, M. Q. (1980). *Qualitative evaluation methods.* Beverly Hills, CA.: Sage Publications.

Pells, E. (2010). *U. of Alabama football's integration legacy revisited, diverse issues in higher education.* Retrieved from http://diverseeducation.com/article/13292/

Perry, T., Steele, C. & Hilliard, A. (2003). *Young, gifted, and African American: promoting high achievement among African American students.* Boston, MA: Beacon Press.

QSR International Pty Ltd. (2011). Retrieved from http://www.qsrinternational.com/what-is-qualitative-research.aspx

Redden, M. (2011). Male students of color from different backgrounds face similar hurdles. *The Chronicle of Higher Education.* June 20, 2011 chronicle.com/article/Male-Students-of-Color-From/127953/

Reiter, M. D., Liput, T, Rashmeen, T. (2007). Personality preferences of college student-athletes. *College Student Journal, 41*(1), 34-36.

Rhoden, W. C. (2008). *Breaking the huddle: The integration of college football.* Retrieved from http://www.hbo.com/sports/breaking-the-huddle-the-integration-of-college-football/index.html

Sack, A. L., & Staurowsky, E. J. (1998). *College athletes for hire.* Westport, CT: Praeger Publishing.

Saylor, R. B. (2011). *African American college football: A brief history: 1930-2004.* LA84 Foundation – Sports Library. http://www.la84foundation.org/SportsLibrary/CFHSN/CFHSNv19/CFHSNv19n1b.pdf

Smith, J.A. (2007). Hermeneutics, human sciences and health: Linking theory and practice. *International Journal of Qualitative Studies on Health and Well-Being, 2,* 3-11

Simiyu, N. W. W. (2009). Triple tragedy of the Black student-athlete. United States Sports Academy. America Sports Academy. The Sports Digest. http://thesportdigest.com/archive/article/triple-tragedy-black-student-athlete.

Sowa, C. J., & Gressard, C. F. (1983). Athletic participation: Relationship to student development. *Journal of College Student Personnel, 24,* 236-239.

Taylor, C. (2005). *Reading through brown eyes: Toward developing a culturally congruent reading curriculum.* Retrieved from http://www.georgiasouthern.edu/etd/archive/fall2005/clara_m_taylor/taylor_clara_m_200508_edd.pdf.

Terragrossa, R. A. (2010). How student achievement is related to student behaviors and learning style preferences. *International Journal of Educational Research, 5*(2). Retrieved from http://www.iabpad.com/IJER/student_achievement.pdf

University of California, Davis. (2006). *A brief introduction to sampling.* Retrieved from http://psychology.ucdavis.edu/rainbow/html/fact_sample.html

Watterson, J. S. (2000). *College football: History, spectacle, controversy.* Baltimore, MD: Johns Hopkins University Press.

Whipple, K. R. (2009), *Athletic identity, identity foreclosure, and career maturity: An investigation of intercollegiate athletes.* Graduate Theses and Dissertations. Paper 10492. http://lib.dr.iastate.edu/etd/10492

Willis, M. G., (2002). Learning styles of African American children; A review of the literature and interventions. *Journal of African American Psychology, 16*(1), 47-65. doi: 10.1177/009579848901600105

Wilson, T. L.Y., Banks, B. A perspective on the education of African American males. *Journal of Instructional Psychology, 21*(1), 97.

APPENDICES

APPENDIX A

Transcriptions of Interviews

Idiographic Approach Researcher's analysis of transcript	**Abraham**: Transcription of interviewer's questions and interviewees answers

1.
 2.
 3.
 4.
 5. Had fun playing football
 6.
 7. Something to do
 8.
 9. Started playing in neighborhood
 10. Mother/ Loved competition
 11.
 12.
 13.
 14. External Motivation
 15.
 16.
 17.
 18.
 19. Competition
 20.
 21. Leadership
 22. Fun
 23. Live in the moment/Ego
 24. Talkative
 25.
 26.
 27.
 28. Debater
 29.
 30. Will listen
 31. Self Actualization
 32. Will speak up
 33. Ego
 34.
 35. Wants success
 36.
 37.
	Interviewer: What uh how long have you played football?
	     Abraham: I played football since I played junior all
	     American
	     I started I'm gonna say 9 10 years old
	 Interviewer: Okay And How did you like it?
	     Abraham: It was, ah, it was it was fun I liked it, it was
	     ah, it fun, it was, I just, I don't know ,it was fun at that
	     time
	     When I was a kid It was you know it was something to
	     do I played Before I played recreational football I
	     played football all of the time on the streets all the time
	     just to do it
	     my mom put me in there I just like competing
	 Interviewer: Oh okay okay so the competition kinda made it even more fun?
	     Abraham: Yeah, It made it more fun
	 Interviewer: So is that something, is that what keeps you motivated sometimes is the competition?
	     Abraham: yeah , yeah
	 Interviewer: Okay, okay, so how do you think other people would describe you?
	     Abraham: like yeah I compete with myself a lot
	     It s like a never ending
	     Ah People would describe me as that's crazy, say as a
	     leader
	     Ah Fun
	     Ah Live in the moment type guy you know
	     But ah, very ah I could be very talkative I guess if I, I
	     don't really notice
	     I started noticing as I got older I was like I could be you

38. Buy mom a house/External Mo	know if I say something
39.	I could be a debater at times you know
40. Success/Ego, Resilience	If I think something is right I probably gonna stick on it
41. Success	But if I know I am wrong I am able to listen also
42.	That's what makes me a cool guy
43. Wealth = Success	If I listen I can speak for myself well
44.	**Interviewer: And then um so what are some of your goals in life?**
45. Thinks of others	Abraham: To be successful I just wanna to be successful
46. Thinks of future self	I wanna be you know
47. Optimistic	**Interviewer: So let…..**
48. High expectation	Abraham: hopefully buy my mom a house you know
49.	what I'm sayin' one day you know what I'm saying
50.	
51.	I want to be successful
52.	That's the only thing I strive for everyday ,success
53.	**Interviewer: Now how do you see success?**
54.	Abraham: First Wealthy
55.	That's what I mean success as
56. Some disappointment in voice	As ah Putting other people on
57.	I want to leave a name for myself
58.	I figure we only live once
59.	I got high expectations
60.	So success is Having enough things grow enough
61	things
62 Some frustration	Not just money but money of course I see that as success but
63	
64	
65	With money I can bring more things around me that's
66	
67	success
68	Wealth not rich
69 Discipline	**Interviewer: Okay great! So then uh are you currently playing football?**
70	
71 Regrets	Doe 1: No
72 Lacked life skill plan	**Interviewer: Okay And then how uh, what importance did it play in your life?**
73	
74 Showing signs of Athletic Identity	Doe 1: Ah
75	**Interviewer: Overall**
76	
77 Life skill planning	

78 Athletic Identity	Abraham: Football to me it pretty much ah is everything
79 No Career Planning	
80	I think it has it good and it has it's bad
81	Ah In football I felt like you know I missed a lot things
82 Andragogy transition	
83	if I wasn't playing football like right now
84 Resourceful	Everything was kinda laid out for me
85	in football once I got to the school
86 Athletic Identity	In pop Warner it was cool like high school once I got to
87 Athletic Identity	
88	high school it was cool
89 Holds on to Athletic Identity	Discipline is the other thing I learned but to the other
90	kind in life
91	If I knew what I knew now
92	I didn't know I also say if I wasn't playing football
93	
94	If I knew what life was all about
95	It kinda blinded me from life being on the football field
96	
97	**Interviewer: Okay Okay Okay**
98	I didn't know you know
99	If football wasn't there you know how would I really
100	
101	survive
102	I always depended on that
103 Low academics – self esteem	And so once it was gone I was kinda like shell shock
104	Oh then now It's like I'm starting all of the way back
105	
106 Possibly ADHD	from in high school
107	When I'm already five years out of here out of there
108 Creative	
109	Because just because of football
110	But when helps me in situations like network if I believe it like
111	
112 Academic issues	When we step into somewhere We always standed out
113 Accommodate deficiencies	
114	because we have that athletic presence
115	we used to in high school we was the man and that
116	carried out through life so that's what I think about
117 Visual learner	
118	football

119
120 Must be relative
121
122 Maturity
123
124
125
126
127 Special Ed – Resource Classes
128
129 Educational Disorientation
130
131
132
133 Lacked Academic Focus
134
135
136 Focus problems
137
138
139
140 Loses interest easily
141
142 Wandering mind
143
144
145
146
147
148
149
150
151
152
153 Lacks focus in life
154
155 Feels life challenges
156
157 Self actualization developing
158 Resilient
	Interviewer: Wow that's interesting. Yea So then uh let me ask you, are you familiar with the term learning style?
	   Abraham: Learning style yea
	Interviewer: What what's your understanding of that?
	   Abraham: I mean, what type of style, what how do you
	   learn
	   The different ways of learning, the different ways of
	   learning
	   I gotta a way different way of learning
	Interviewer: So what how do you understand what is your learning, what is your learning style?
	   Abraham: Learning just anything?
	Interviewer: anything
	   Abraham: just anything
	   My learning style
	   I don't know I never been that smart I guess
	   My attention span is very short sometimes I just bounce
	   around bounce around and think all day bout a million
	   different things And then like, even when I listen,
	   I was just telling my him my friend
	   I can only listen then images start popping up in my
	   heard
	   so that's what I learn my learning style
	   So it's kind of funny
	   Even with me with words like
	   I was really taught how to sound to spell words out
	   I use my imagination and figure out how it looks
	   That's how I learned all of my words
	Interviewer: so you're saying you're sorta like a visual? a visual learner?
	   Abraham: Yeah a visual learner
	Interviewer: What I'm hearing you say is you have a couple of things going, you're a visual

159	learner but you also uh need to uh be able to relate to it.
160	
161	Abraham: Right right
162 Uses sports to stabilize - restless	**Interviewer: so ah you have some insight, so how have you used, Let me back up a minute, I heard you say that you weren't that smart. what's your definition of smart?**
163 Competitive	
164 Success	
165	Abraham: I never I didn't mean that's what I never been
166	
167	as smart as pretty much the others in the class
168	I was a, when I was coming up, I had resource classes
169	
170	I couldn't like People get done with their test fast
171 Not in college	It would mess me up, I couldn't get things, it would take
172	
173	me a little more time
174	Sometimes I just felt like I couldn't get it all period
175	
176	But I can get it in a different you know
177	I could listen to a teacher and I don't know what they
178 Adult learning ready	
179 May learn better now	sayin
180	Everything it's, is starting, it's just like the music
181	everything just started fading out
182	I try to stay focused
183 Life happened	Sometimes my mind you know wonders off
184	Just like the music
185	I could only listen to it for so long
186 Reflection – life skills	Especially if I'm not interested in it
187	**Interviewer: where does it wonder off to?**
188	Abraham: Whatever else I am thinking about
189 Optimistic	**Interviewer: is it related in anyway? Is it totally different?**
190	
191	Abraham: Probably not Probably not, totally different.
192	
193	**Interviewer: So now it seems that you have a really good awareness of how you learn, which is good. So how do you apply that to life?**
194	
195 Finances	
196	
197 School is secondary	Abraham: ah Let's see ah It's kind of like that's what I
198	explained that's kind of where I am with my life
199	You know I'm everywhere, I bounce around here and
200	
201	there.

202	If I could just you know probably just slow it down a
203 Reflection – life skills	little more
204 Reflection – being independent	I'm still adapting to this life thing
205 Athletic Identity	I'm still trying to become so
206	Right now I know who I am
207 Mother enabled - unknowing	I still tryin to better to who I am
	That's how I think I'm just bouncing around
208 Reflection – being independent	So How do I apply that to life
	I'm Trying to think
209	I uh I use sports too back to my sports
210	I use my competitive side
211	And my strive to success
212 Reflection – not prepared for life	Every day I try to better myself and that's how I did in
213	sports
214	What kept me going was always to be successful
215	I use the football I use my sports
216	In my life a lot
217 No prepared interested in college	**Interviewer: so if you ah, first of all are you in college right**
218 On line college but willing to	**now?**
	Abraham: No
219 Consider it	**Interviewer: If you were to go back to college, uh, would you stay longer if you had classes that addressed you style of learning? Because it sounds like you are a multi-tasker, you have to be doing more than one thing at one time. So if you had a class that taught that way, do you think you would it would be easier for you to get through school?**
220	
221	
222	
223	
224	
225	
226 Music is more important	Abraham: Yeah un uh
	Yeah I'm not gonna
227	I think if I got back in school now I would way better
228	
229	I think just Because I a better understanding of myself
230	
231	
232	Like I said back then the sports took me
233 Pipe Dreams	Reality hit me
234	I was kind of blind to it
235	If I went back now I think I , I think I, but
236 People person	To answer your questions That would help me
237	I not one to make too many excuses
238	Because that's pretty much what life is all about

239	You get obstacles all the time
240 Wants to help people	So if I went back now I believe I could stay longer
241	
242	But Now I in this so that's another thing
243	**Interviewer: what do you mean this**
244	Abraham: Unh?
245	**Interviewer: you said this**
246	Abraham: Now I'm in debt
247 Music goal	**Interviewer: oh**
248 Communicator	Abraham: I can't go back to school right now so
249 Music = Journalism	Now I got a job and I'm working
250 Helper	I wish I would have had a job when I was in school
251	
252	**Interviewer: So um, so that's one of the things that if you had to do it over again, if you had to prepare for college again, what would you do different?**
253 Business goals	
254	
255 Entrepreneurship	
256	Abraham: Uhh take more initiative in doing a lot of
257 Focused on music	
258 Leadership skills	things
259	Getting a lot of things done from my stand point
260	Not depend on others to do it
261 Helping others	I came in an let coaches handle that
262 Analogy provided	My mom give me this in the dorm rooms
263	And I should have just taken the initiatives to do things
264	
265	I should of did for myself so therefore I would know
266	
267	what I
268	was doing
269	So when it all feel down me I knew from the jump
270	
271 Reality escape	So that everything wasn't just a surprise
272	So that's what I would have did.
273	**Interviewer: So you know a lot of colleges now, you have like on line colleges and ah where you can start and stop whenever you want, how would that work for you?**
274	
275 Athletic Identity vs Academic	
276 ID	Abraham: It would it would I think I could do it
277	It just a point of whether I wanted to do it
278	If I didn't want to do it then I probably wouldn't do it
279	
280 No history known of football	If I want to do it than I would get it done
	So on line classes

281	I'd have to see what class I was taking
282	What am I doing I have to want to do it
283	**Interviewer: What are your interest in life? What are your plans for the future?**
284 Sports – heart felt	
285	Abraham: I want to start I want to do music
286	I want to start my own business
287 Competition	I want to start my own record company
288 Works with others	I'm an entrepreneur
289 Discipline	I want to build everything from the ground up
290 Only child	I want to create a whole village once I leave
291 Identity	**Interviewer: wow**
292	Abraham: I wanna start from the, I wanna piece
293	of this
294	If I had a village I want lots of houses around
295	With all of my friends around to the point that I just
296 Other football student-athletes admired	keep going.
297	That's how I dream
298 ADHD Behavior continued	If I'm going to leave I want a big house
	I want a lot of big houses
299	I want all of my friends around me, I figure we
300	just keep
301	going.
302	I figure if I dream big I can get close to it that's
303	cool.
304	**Interviewer: so That's a lot first of all, I mean**
305	**you can do it. Your young enough you know but**
306	**it requires steps. I always say baby steps. So**
307	**when you're looking at baby steps?**
308 Like dissertation subject	Abraham: My music
	is just a way so that I will be able to talk to the
309	people
310	I look at music as a way of journalism
311	I can tell people how I feel
312	I can tell people about their situations
313	Once I start that and
314	Make a mogul out of myself
315	Music is just a part of it
316	I want to more of a entrepreneur than an artist
317 Will ask questions for clarity	That's just the first step
	If I can get my music out there and
318	I can be able to change other people's situations
319	out
320	there

321	That are similar to mine
322	Telling my story I end up telling someone else's
323	story
324	Helping others
325	I always say I'll take a million people before I
326	take a
327	Million dollars
328	If I got a million people in the back of me a
329	million
330	dollars ain't nothing.
331	I can got a dollar from each of them I'll have a
332	million
333	dollars.
334	**Interviewer: Very interesting, I like the way you**
335	**think. I really do. So let me just ask you another**
336	**question, and this is going back to football, um,**
337	**what is your knowledge as far as football for the**
338	**African American male?**
339	Abraham: It's a Scapegoat
340	When I was first coming I was really ah my mind
341	my
342 **Important point**	mom wasn't as wealthy as she is now. It was
343	something
344 In agreement	to do.
345 Life skills	I looked at it I wasn't the smartest like I said
346	If I could play football good enough I would
347 Feelings of being	have to
unprepared	worry about the other stuff I could just make it
348	off of
349 Agrees with other	my skills.
football	**Interviewer: do did Were you ever taught the**
350 student-athletes having	**history of football as far as how the African**
the same	**American came to be involved in it?**
351 problem	Abraham: Nah
352	**Interviewer: Do you think that if you knew the**
353	**impact of how it came to be where it is now,**
354	**would it have made a difference to you?**
355	Abraham: Nah not really because I love doing it I
356	love
357	going out there
358	I still kinda miss it this day
359	I love going out there competing strapping up
360	That why I work well with others
361	I learned discipline working with others

362	I was the only child
363	Football was a reason to be around my brothers
364	I loved that feeling going out there and riding with my
365	boys
366 Feels like there is a need for	I still love that to this day
367 more studies	**Interviewer: Do you have any football student-athletes that you**
368	**idolized?**
369	Abraham: Deon Sanders Jerry Rice Steve Young Troy
370	Akins
371	
372	
373	**Interviewer: Did you ever study their styles and model them?**
374	
375	Abraham: Every time I watched a game I could never
376 Wants to finish college	finish watching it because I wanted to go out there and
377	play
378 Obligated to athletic values	That's how I pretty much studied, I had to go out there
379	and play.
380 Feels internal unresolved	Yeah so Yea
381 issues	**Interviewer: oh okay that's good that's good you said you were a visual learner so that makes sense, that makes sense. Anything you want to talk about that you think would be beneficial as far as my subject matter?**
382	
383	
384	
385	
386 Was almost finished college	Abraham: It's actually a good subject matter too
387	I meant to tell you about that
388	Uh
389	You pretty much touched everything though, you pretty
390	much touched everything
391 Wants to go back to college	But ah,
392	What are yall trying to do like ah
393	Yall tryin to find just
394 Can't commit to going to	Explain it again?
395 school full time, interested	**Interviewer: Okay see this is what I want to do, I'm telling you are giving me really good information I am really excited I excited to hear what comes from everyone else I interview but my whole goal is to develop a teaching method**
396 in music now	
397	
398 Has good work ethics	

399	for athletes because athletes I have my own idea I
400	don't know but I used to be an athlete myself.
401	Abraham: Ok
402	**Interviewer: so I have an idea myself but not**
403 People person	**from a male perspective.**
404	Abraham: Un unh
405	**Interviewer: so um what I would like to do is you**
406	**know um how in school you have majors.**
407 Mostly works and	Abraham: Un unh
promotes his	**Interviewer: I don't know if they have this as**
408 music	**much now but like clerical you would get classes**
409	**geared toward clerical.**
410	Abraham: Ok
411	**Interviewer: if you wanted to be an attorney or**
412	**go into the legal field then they would try to give**
413	**you classes especially in high school that would**
414 Still needs to be among	**help you with that**
people	Abraham: Oh ok
415	**Interviewer: so for athletes, there's nothing**
416	Abraham: oh ok
417	**Interviewer: athlete, my thought is an athlete**
418	**should be**
419	**trained to be an athlete**
420	Abraham: yeah yeah
421	Abraham and Interviewer: On the field and off
422 Minimal Ed. Planning	the field
for	yeah
423 business	**Interviewer: that's what I think**
424	Abraham: And it think that is missing
425	Teach a athlete how to be a man
426	If you really gonna say he a student-athlete
427	Then make sure he's a student-athlete and not
428	just an
429	athlete
430	Sometimes you got friends that go to the league
431 Focus on music and	to that
business	I know some friends that I got that are in the
432	NFL, they
433	still behind you know
434	**Interviewer: right and that's why I think you it's**
435 Creative	**like people who come from astute backgrounds,**
436	**it's like people that have money, well, they are**
437	**trained how to handle money from day one**
438	Abraham: um umm

439 Music = Journalism
440
441
442
443
444 Music writer
445
446
447
448
449
450
451
452
453
454
455
456
457
458
459
460
461
462
463
464
465
466
467
468
469
470
471
472
473
474
475
476
477
478
479
480
481
482
	Interviewer: athletes should be taught to handle their money as well as their talent from day one. So if your mind is that you're going to be a professional athlete, you should be learning how to read contracts, leaning how to invest money, learning anger management, learning how to handle stress, you know all of those things need to be part of the package so that you don't try to learn it all when you become 18 years old that's what I'm looking at.
	    Abraham: Yeah
	    That's a smart idea
	Interviewer: Yeah so that's what I looking at
	    Abraham: Hopefully I can help I helped a little bit
	Interviewer: You helped tremendously, you helped tremendously. Like I said that you have really good insight as to where you are now, it sounds like you have good insight , you just need help to get to the next level. I sure that will happen also. I do want to ask you though, do you intend to return to college at some point?
	    Abraham: Yeah
	    I definitely want to finish
	    I started it
	    That's the one thing always Sports taught me not to
	    quite.
	    That's going to be in the back of my mind regardless if I
	    wanted to be there or not
	Interviewer: and you got how far in college, how many, how many years?
	    Abraham: Three years
	Interviewer: three years, so you would be going back for how long?
	    Abraham: Probably A year and some change
	Interviewer: so let's see you are how old right now?
	    Abraham: 23
	Interviewer: so do you see yourself going back within the next two years?
	    Abraham: Yea definitely

483	**Interviewer: ah would you see yourself going**
484	**back full time or part time?**
485	Abraham: Part-time
486	Just because hopefully other things will start
487	panning
488	out too
489	**Interviewer: now Tell me some of the other**
490	**things you're doing right now?**
491	Abraham: Working trying to get as much money
492	as
493	possible to provide for my business ventures that
494	I want
495	to get into
496	**Interviewer: And you told me you were working**
497	**before I put you on tape recorder**
498	Abraham: I'm a bartender at a hotel
499	Networking with people there and working on
500	my
501	People working on my communication skills
502	**interviewer: and then your other ventures right**
503	**now are?**
504	Abraham: Music
505	That's it Working and music
506	I'm trying to build my music which is Zue Krew
507	We all feel like we didn't have nothing but
508	bosses
509	I feel like everyone is different
510	Everyone has their own thing
511	You only live once try to live it to the best of
512	your
513	Ability.
514	And so That's what I'm working on
515	My other friends have other things going on
516	Got restaurants
517	Got Videos
518	If we all put it together we will become even
519	bigger
520	**Interviewer: now you say that ah you say that ah**
521	**people say that to really get a good grasp of what**
522	**your planning. You really need to study how**
523	**things operate. Even though you are not in**
524	**college are you doing some self help things too.**
525	Abraham: I read a couple books I haven't been
526	reading

527	lately but I read a couple of books
528	I read a Huey P Newton the spirit of the panther
529	and a
530	Hill Hartford that was probably like a year ago,
531	"A
532	Letter to a African American Man."
533	**Interviewer: I'm familiar with that book**
534	Abraham: I read the jay z book he's a rap artists
535	So I do a little bit
536	**Interviewer: okay**
537	Abraham: I'm marketing music.
538	All the thoughts that come into my head I try to get
539	
540	them out.
541	I have a lot of thoughts all day
542	I can only get them out at certain times because I have
543	
544	to work.
545	I just right until I pass out
546	**Interviewer: so your write music as well as rap it? okay**
547	
548	Abraham: But I'm writing I write like I said
549	Music is a part of journalism
550	So of course I have to watch, if I was talking about
551	
552	sports I have to watch little sports
553	if I'm going to talk about whets going on in the world
554	
555	I have to watch the new CNN
556	I keep myself update
557	I try to get my thoughts in there to explain
	Interviewer: okay that's what I was going to ask you about, to see if you were watching videos or television. So that's good well I know we have been talking for a while okay I know we have been talking for a while this is the end of interview one.

Idiographic Approach Researcher's analysis of transcript	**Martin**: Transcription of interviewer's questions and interviewees answers

1.
 2. Played since early childhood
 3. Started at eight years old
 4.
 5.
 6.
 7.
 8.
 9.
 10.
 11. Liked the sport
 12.
 13.
 14.
 15.
 16.
 17.
 18. Hardworker
 19. Determined
 20.
 21. Cool Guy
 22. Well rounded
 23. Hardworking
 24.
 25.
 26.
 27. Business minded
 28.
 29. Selling hair
 30.
 31. Restaurnant owner
 32.
 33.
 34.
 35. Real Estate
 36.
 37. Future football coach
 38.
 39. Business ownership
 40.
	Interviewer: How long have you played football?
	       Martin: I been playing football for probably about
	       sixteen years, since
	       I was eight years old. A little while.
	 Interviewer: Ok so you started as, ah, what as pop, ah, I can't remember .
	       Martin: Rialto ah Junior All American Pop Warner
	 Interviewer: pop Warner ok?
	       Martin: yeah yeah
	 interviewer: okay and how did you like it?
	       Martin: I liked it I loved it
	        I mean My first year it was okay
	        I was kind of chunky
	        So I played on line but I still I just liked being out
	         there so
	 Interviewer: and ah so if I were if I were to ask someone to describe you right now, how do you think people would describe you?
	       Martin: They would describe me as Hard working and
	       determined
	       Definitely those two
	       Fairly I'm Cool guy just you know nice to talk to
	       Well rounded
	       But pretty much hard working though
	       You know I m always trying u know to make it happen so
	 Interviewer: and then um so, can you tell me some of the goals you have in life right now?
	       Martin: Right now ah Right now I have a I'm working
	       on having a couple of businesses
	       One is the hair business
	       I sell hair "her hair"
	       And then I also ah plan on opening a restaurant so

41. Not playing football right now	within the next year
42.	So I like the restaurant industry that whole thing
43.	I also want to get into real estate
44.	Buying and selling you know houses and things like
45.	
46.	that
47.	And ah Few other things
48. Visual learner	Like I want to get back in to maybe coaching football
49.	
50.	and stuff like that
51.	But really just business ownership
52.	**Interviewer: okay so are you playing football right now?**
53.	
54.	Martin: Nah I played my last year I played was 010,
55.	
56.	2010 yeah
57.	**Interviewer: and ah you know I talked about uh learning styles, are you familiar with that term?**
58.	
59.	Martin: Ummmmm I prob I heard it before
60.	but I not really sure of what exactly it entitles
61.	**Interviewer: ok well do you know have you ever thought about how you learn?**
62.	
63.	Martin: I would probably say I am more of a visual
64.	
65.	learner
66.	I like to see it
67. Visual and Kinesthetic learner	I'm sorry I have to get this call
	Interviewer: don't worry about it
68.	Martin: Excuse me (stopped to take a phone call)
69.	
70. Reads and writes info down	hello……
	This girl is trying to get some hair, I'm sorry
71.	**Interviewer: that's ok you just told me you were a business man right so you know**
72.	
73.	Martin: Yeah I'm trying to make it happen
74.	**Interviewer: yeah you know this is the way that's how**
75.	
76.	**business men operate**
77.	Martin: Yeah yeah
78.	**Interviewer: and that you know not that I was trying to listen to your conversation but I was listening to how you were conducting and so I was I was impressed**
79.	
80.	
81.	

82. Makes an agenda – organ skills
83.
84.
85. Researchs internet for info
86. Self development
87.
88. Understands the need for
89. education in college
90.
91. Major/Radio Television Film
92. Use of kinesthetic learning style
93.
94. Major relates to learning style
95. Applies learned behavior to life 96. skill
97.
98.
99.
100.
101.
102. Senior in college
103. Sched to graduate in one sem
104.
105.
106.
107.
108.
109.
110.
111.
112.
113.
114.
115. Life includes a 3 yr old dau
116.
117.
118.
119.
	Martin: Thank you
	Interviewer: and so um but we were discussing learning styles and my question was what your learning style and you said that you thought it were a visual learner
	    Martin: Yeah visual learner and probably more of like
	    a repetitive learner like the more I do it the better
	    obviously the more you do it the better you get but
	    If I read something and then read it again and
	    probably write it down and read it again I am able to
	    get it as opposed to just seeing it one time
	    So I mean probably a little bit of both
	Interviewer: so you are a little visual and what they call kinesthetic
	    Martin: Yes
	Interviewer: so that good so ah having an idea of what your learning styles are how do you apply it to your everyday life and school?
	    Martin: Um Well I mean I guess really I use I do like
	    every day I make sure
	    Like I have a little agenda that I'll write and I just I
	    just do it
	    I mean As far as my learning style I mean and how I
	    apply it to my daily life
	    I mean Everyday I'm always googling and trying to
	    look up something like learning about this hair or
	    different looking up different industries
	    I need to know about entrepreneurship
	    Plus I mean I'm in school
	    So I'm learning everyday as far as just being in class
	    listening
	    My major right now is RTF.
	    So It's a lot of hands on stuff so it's not really a lot of

120.
121.
123.
124.
125.
126.
127. Knows something about AA
128. football history but not much
129.
130.
131.
132.
133.
134.
135.
136.
137.
138.
139.
140. Not sure if knowledge matters,
141. believes it may have had some
142. impact
143.
144. Athletic identity already set in
145. high school
146.
147.
148.
149.
150. High academics
151. Father encouraged good grades
152.
153.
154.
155. Negl investigation regarding
156. math requirements for college
	writing .
	Interviewer: Now what is RTF?
	    Martin: Radio television and film
	    So I'm like real good at
	    I'm trying to be a movie director
	    I also am like doing videos media and nearly anything that has to do with media so
	Interviewer: okay so you are still in college?
	    Martin: Yes
	Interviewer: in what year are you in college right now?
	    Martin: I'm in my senior year
	    I got maybe a semester left I'll bout to graduate soon
	Interviewer: fabulous very good so you're in school so you um you're just um more of just a student now and not a student athlete?
	    Martin: Yeah
	    (interrupted by woman coming into the room)
	    Did you call me?
	Interviewer: hold on one second that's okay you know what I'm trying to figure out how to put this on hold but I not having doing real good so I just want to let you know hi, that were recording so just so you know I guess this is your life this is your life
	    Martin: Yeah this is my life
	    This is the mother of my child
	    Yeah
	Interviewer: so I'm good I'm good
	    Martin: thank you Yes
	Interviewer: and she's cute by the way she's cute yea she's very cute so um so um right now you say you've given up the student part I mean the athlete part and that's good I'm glad to see your still moving forward um what do you know about the history of football as far as when African Americans became involved in it?
	    Martin: ummmm I really wouldn't say I know too
	    much about the history of football of African
	    American I know about the story of Jim brown and
	    some of the

157.	Things he went through to play for Syracuse you
158.	know
159.	He's one of the first African American guys like I have heard
160. NCAA clearinghouse issues	stories but as far as the actual history I'm not too sure
161. Current college assisted him	about it I haven't really heard
162.	**Interviewer: so if you were taught the history of football do you think it would have made any difference in how you handled the sport? And when I say history, I keep saying history, but more of the history of African American involvement.**
163.	
164. Critical to know how the sports	
165. business works	
166.	
167.	
168.	Martin: Ummmmmm probably not and
169. In a home where ed was a	If I did know the history it probably would have
170. priority	made me work even harder just knowing that we had
171.	it harder
172.	So I mean it probably would have helped if anything
173. strong father figure in house	a little bit
174. who emphasized education	I was already in the all in football you know
175.	that was my whole life eat sleep dream Monday thru
176.	Friday
177. motivated to be educated in order	my dream that's what I thought about all day so
178. for better sports opportunity	**Interviewer: okay so then if you had to prepare for college again, uh is there anything you would have done differently relative to being a student-athlete?**
179.	
180.	
181.	
182.	Martin: The only thing that I would have done
183.	differently is because of my academic was actually
184.	
185.	pretty good
186. current lifestyle is very busy	My father is was on my I was no way there was no
187.	way that I couldn't bring home nothing less than a B
188. multi tasker	
189. different things going on	so I graduated with high honors with a 3.8
190.	But what I didn't do is to go through the NCAA

191. business, school, co-parenting	clearinghouse on the athletic side so that's what
192.	disqualified me from being eligible to play for a lot of
193.	
194. focused on business ventures	the division one colleges
195.	It wasn't like it disqualified me it's that a lot of the
196. preparing for better life for dau	Bigger schools they expect you to already be in the
197.	NCAA clearinghouse as opposed to some of the
198.	
199.	smaller schools like TSU they'll accept you and kinda
200. sells hair, hats, t-shirts	help you get through it and all that so as far as the
201. photography	
202. videos, etc.	paper work, I would just be more in tune to what the
203.	
204.	paperwork and the logistic side of being a NCAA
205.	
206.	athlete.
207.	**Interviewer: so what it sounds like is so what it sounds like is even though you were a student-athlete in high school, the focus was more on education than the sport**
208.	
209.	
210.	
211.	
212.	Martin: In my household yea
213. best advice, know what you're	it was all about school and then
	It was definitely work hard in football for sure
214. getting into when you go to	That was what I probably would have chose
	But just based on what my father and how he was
215. play sports in college	
216.	you know how he was,
217.	it was like you know school first and then get good
218. lots of politicking in college	grades it would be a lot easier for you play football
219.	
220. things go wrong that are not	and go to the school you want to go to
	So that was always my motivation
221. publicized	**Interviewer: so then would one of your preparations then be for if you had to do it over again would be to have a little more knowledge of what is needed to be an athlete and a student in college on both levels as a student and an athlete**
222.	
223.	
224. Coaches get fired	
225.	
226. Stay clear of temptations	
	Martin: Yeah

227.	**Interviewer: okay um so if I walked around in your world, what would it look like to me.**
228. Stud ath/not supposed	Martin: It would look kind of crazy only because I
229. to accept anythng frm anybody	have a lot of things going on
230.	I have my hands dipped in a lot of different you know
231. Exceptd something but didn't	Just got a lot of different things going on
232. get in trouble, didn't know not	As far as three different businesses I have my hair
233.	business
234.	I'm going to school and trying to be a good father
235. Got in trouble by assoc with	Trying to do it all
236. a certain coach.	It be cool
237. Good athlete	I don't do too much because I'm really all about
238.	business right now.
239.	I want to be ready for her.
240.	It's easy now but girls I know they can get expensive
241.	**Interviewer: you have three businesses so what are your businesses**
242	Martin: I sell hair and then I also sell hats and t-shirts
243.	and I also have a photography business
244.	I do like different Portfolios, and I also do videos,
245.	like music videos and editing and a bunch of little
246.	stuff.
247.	**Interviewer: oh so you really can fix my camera**
248. Four year varsity letterman	Martin: I don't know if I can fix it but I can probably
249. Felt work in high school/ for	operate it a little
250. nothing	AJ he can fix it he can probably dissect the whole
251. Be aware because some people	thing.
252. have the wrong motives	He's really my engineer but I can operate it a little bit
253.	though.
254.	**Interviewer: well is there anything that you can**
255.	
256.	
257.	
258.	
259.	
260.	
261.	**add to what I've talked to you about that would**
262.	
263.	**help when we are looking at African American**

264.	**male learning styles or just that would motivate you or any other roadblock that would come up**
265.	
266. Make school your priority	Martin: Making sure that you know what you're
267.	getting into and you know what you have to do to get
268.	
269.	there don't think I'm just gonna play football
270. Believes that education is the	don't just go to school
	It's a lot more to it
271. yet	It's a lot of politics I ran into a lot of politics
272. to more opportunities in	But just know it's more to it than school and football
273. football	
274.	There's paperwork to sign
275.	People get in trouble for stuff that everyday people
276.	
277	don't even hear about
278	There's a lot of things that go on in the colleges
279	
280	Like in football you know coaches getting fired for
281	
282	doing stuff
283	You just gotta make sure that you stay clear of all of
284	
285	the temptations there is a lot of stuff that even I fell
286	
287	victim to.
288	**Interviewer: um um ok can you elaborate?**
289	Martin: Just like pretty much I was I accepted some
290	
291	stuff you know
292	Really As a student-athlete you not really supposed to
293	
294	accept certain stuff
295	In my case I never got in trouble for my stuff but my
296	
297	coach got caught for something else but it was just
298	
299	that because I was part of that class I was just….
300	
301	**Interviewer: by association?**
302	Martin: Yes I was associated with it and so
303	I kinda fell victim to
304	I really was a good athlete
305	I was four year varsity lettermen in high school

    I did all that work and get behind a coach and me not
    knowing it okay I shouldn't take that
    Be aware of what's going on
    Always know people's motives its always motives

Interviewer: so then okay what I like that because it sounds like what your saying is that one of the things I'm looking at is the student-athlete in high school taking a class on how to be a student-athlete in college or if you don't go to college how to be an athlete part of it is really important as far as the actual class on the guidelines for being a student-athlete

    Martin: Yea

Interviewer: I like that very good, ok well if there is nothing else you would like to add you have given me some really good information anything else that you think would be beneficial?

    Martin: That's pretty much it coming from my perspective
    School is most important
    I seen a lot of athletes get washed away
    I was a decent student-athlete but because I was always on
    honor roll I could get at least that try out
    If you don't get the grades you can't gonna get the try
    out. That's about it.

Idiographic Approach Researcher's analysis of transcript	John: Transcription of interviewer's questions and interviewees answers
1.	**Interviewer: So let's start with how long have you played football?**
2.	
3. played six years	John: About ah six years
4.	**Interviewer: Six years and how important is football to your life?**
5.	
6.	John: Actually about right now it's not
7.	
8.	important at all but during time me playing
9. played baseball also	
10.	the game it was probably the only thing I
11.	
12. played sports most of life	was thinking about besides my secondary
13.	
14.	sport which was baseball
15. described as a big teddy bear	**Interviewer: So you, sports took a good portion of your life as you were growing up?**
16. beast on the field	
17. good honest caring good friend	
18.	John: Yeah pretty much yeah a great portion
19. beast on the field (proud of it)	
20.	**Interviewer: ok so if I asked someone to describe you, how do you think they would describe you?**
21.	
22. concerned about being able to sup family	
23.	John: They would describe me as the big
24. wants to help others	teddy bear that played that was a beast on
25.	
26.	the field baby face you know they always
27. entrepreneurship	
28. searching for self	say that and
29.	Good honest caring person type good friend
30.	
31. sells hair,	beast on the field though
32. does photography, edit videos, music	**Interviewer: what about your goals in life, what about your goals for the future?**
33.	
34.	John: Overall goals is to have enough
35. trying to sell Nestle products	money to be able to take care of me and my
36. trying to start a business	
37.	family and whoever else that might need
38.	
39.	some money on the way uh and that's
40.	pretty much it

41.	However whichever way I go of course I'm
42.	an entrepreneur so I'm trying to get into a
43.	little bit of everything just to see what's my
44.	niche
45.	**Interviewer: so what kind of entrepreneurship ventures are you in right now?**
46. Has a business plan for two businesses	
47.	
48.	
49.	
50.	John: Currently selling hair also well I
51. Not currently playing football	started a little, do photography, got a new
52.	camera so, I started doing ah little editing
53.	
54.	
55.	videos, music videos I'm starting to do a
56.	little production and I also started selling
57.	
58.	
59. Thinking about playing baseball/recreation	Nestle products I'm starting to getting a
60.	little business started with that
61.	**Interviewer: What product is that?**
62.	John: Nestle
63.	**Interviewer: What is that?**
64.	John: Ice cream they also bought out
65.	D'Giornos pizza California pizza kitchen
66. Familiar with learning styles	
67.	pizza things like that
68.	**Interviewer: Okay interesting so what have you done at this point to start putting those others in place like do you have business plans or ?**
69.	
70. Able to define it adequately	
71.	
72.	John: Well not for everything I have business
73.	
74.	plans for two of the things, the hair
75.	adventure and the production but as far as
76.	
77.	the others no there's no business plan in
78. Visual learner	place yet
79.	**Interviewer: ok so are you currently playing base… playing football?**
80.	
81. Memorizes information	
82.	John: No

135

83. 84. Lots of things from memory 85. 86. 87. 89. 90. 91. 92. 93. 94. 95. 96. College was challenging 97. Found he needed to change learning style 98. The information was not always presented 99. on the board 100. Questions not always answered/detail 101. 102. College required more independent study 103. 104. 105. 106. You had to study in order to keep up 107. 108. 109. 110. Learning styles worked for high school 111. 112. 113. Knew part/what required for college 114. 115. 116. 117. Lower class college classes worked 118. learning style	**Interviewer: Are you playing any sports at all because I know you said you played more than one sport** 　　John: No I'm thinking about it but not such 　　as now no **Interviewer: ok what sport are you thinking about playing?** 　　John: Well I was trying to look for a little 　　baseball league some Sunday baseball league 　　just to get out there 　　See what's good, get my swing back 　　Just play around get a little shape **Interviewer: ok so now are you familiar with the term learning styles** 　　John: Well yea I've heard of learning styles, 　　different learning styles before **Interviewer: okay so what's your understanding of what that is?** 　　John: Uh shoot probably I guess just pretty 　　much everybody has different learning styles we might see the same things 　　but keep it in your mind a different way 　　It might stick with you a little better 　　so everybody is different **Interviewer: so what do you think your learning style is?** 　　John: I think I'm more of a visual person 　　Listening I might get bored and 　　then I might think about some other stuff 　　But looking at it my eyes are going to be 　　glued to it and I'm going to remember everything I just saw that's pretty much, 　　that's pretty much how I learn 　　A lot of things by memory,

119. He was challenged to think/ became 120. a problem for him 121. 122. 123. Problems really started in college once he 124. wasn't playing football anymore 125. 126. 127. 128. 129. 130. Resources/available to him at college 131. Did not take advantage of opportunity 132. 133. 134. 135. Pre-occupied/things other than college 136. 137. Football team was not doing well which 138. affected his ability to do well in college 139. because other students were not happy 140. with the team which made him mad. He 141. would have to listen to their criticism 142. when he went to class. 143. 144. 145. 146. 147. 148. 149. 150. 151.	remembering and seeing what I saw and then putting down the answer down that's how I do stuff **Interviewer: so have you applied your learning styles to being a student-athlete?** John: Like ah whatcha mean like? **interviewer: well you know you have an idea as to what your learning styles are so when you're in school, do you, how do learn while you're in school?** John: School is pretty well college was kinda hard to learn for looking because they might have it on there but they go through it pretty fast you can ask a question and try to figure it out but they not gonna spend too much time on it its gonna be you it's strictly gonna be you it some after school stuff, some after class stuff to study to stay abreast of what's going on **Interviewer: so as a student-athlete how did you yourself then?** John: During high school I thought I did pretty well as a student-athlete being able to get through school it wasn't my main main focus but I knew I had to pass it to get to where I wanted to get to which was to play freshman sports but in college it worked for a little while but after I got into the upper level it didn't really work as

152. Athletic Identity	well and
153.	then I didn't really adapt to what I really
154. Planning to return to college in the fall 2012	needed to do to pass
155.	**Interviewer: what do you think would have been helpful to you once you got in college?**
156.	
157.	
158.	John: Well I think my problems were was
159.	
160. No knowledge of AA football integrat	once I wasn't play in the sports would when I was playing sports
161.	I think it probably would have been helpful,
162.	
163.	hold on do you mean to be able to stay in
164.	
165.	school, to continue?
166.	**Interviewer: um um**
167.	John: Everything was really pretty much in
168.	
169.	place
170.	I just really didn't take advantage of the
171. Knowledge might have helped some.	opportunities to to get further
172.	**Interviewer: and what do you think was preventing you from taking advantage of it?**
173.	
174.	
175.	John: I'm thinking about other stuff
176.	Trying to think about , Not school pretty
177.	
178.	much,
179.	I'm thinking about the team and about how
180.	
181.	we ain't winning no games
182.	I don't even want to go to class and cain't be
183.	
184.	proud about being on the team because we
185.	
186. Feels like he gave his all to football	ain't' doing nothin'
187.	I always had to go to class about people
188.	
189.	talking about the football team and
190. Growing pains	I can't just let them talk about the football
191. Working hard and thinking	team

192. 193. 194. Worried about finances 195. 196. 197. Working on being more self supportive 198. 199. 200. 201. Wants to be able to help others 202. 203. 204. 205. 206. Parents are encouraging him 207. 208. Knows a college education is important 209. Believes he can do well w/o a college ed. 210. 211. 212. Wants to finish what he started. 213. 214. Motivation is his parents. 215. 216. 217. Sees college degree as a good back up 218. 219. Believes that a college degree doesn't 220. promise a job. 221. 222. 223. Time/ wasted whether you go to college 224. or not. 225. 226. 227. 228.	There was a lot of distractions, a lot of distractions The ladies you know that was a distraction as well once you get in college **Interviewer: and so you were having a problem really focusing on academics because everything was , the athletics was and anything relating to it was distracting? Is that what you're saying?** John: A lot more glamorous than the books **Interviewer: so um so are in college right now?** John: No but I am trying to get back in for the fall. **Interviewer: ok and then can I ask you a question about ah, there is a history with African American football student-athletes, are you familiar with how African American football student-athletes became part of football ? the integration part of it?** John: No I don't know too much or nothing about the integration of football or the African American man I know I seen where they talk about it briefly but the history no **Interviewer: well would that had made a difference if you knew about the history and how African Americans became a part of the football teams and the affect of it if you knew of it and how it really became to be as it is now, would it have made a difference of how you looked at participated in that sport?** Doe 3: It could have if I was coming up in that age

229.	You know they just really had something to
230.	fight for and not just taken it as a given
231. Ethnic identification – AA more driven	it's like this is here and that's what we are
232.	supposed to play
233.	me not knowing the history I guess it would
234. History – negative for AA	make a difference to know that
235.	we kind of blessed to have been able to play
236.	football
237. AA motivated to	Me personally it might
238. succeed because they are AA	It might just not make a difference to me
239. system against the AA	It might of affected me a little
240.	But just knowing it would be good but it
241.	might not just knowing it is good
242.	I might not just affect me on the field because
243. Motivated because AA and neg history	I already gave all I had on the field
244.	so it was like whatever
245.	**Interviewer: so tell me what I would see if I walked around in your world?**
246.	John: Ups and downs shoot uh
247.	A lot of hard work lot of thinking
248. Strength in the motivation	A lot of thinking
249.	**Interviewer: what do you think about?**
250.	John: Thinking about the next way to get
251.	that next dollar trying to get mo money
252.	Trying to get some money
253.	So that I can be comfortable and
254.	have my own space
255. Success – based on who you know	To be able to continue on my own
256.	Not have to have help
257.	To be able to help other people that would
258. Top schools/top of class/no difference	need help
259.	**Interviewer: so I heard you say that you're going back to college what's motivating you at this point to go back to college?**
260.	
261. Network development is important	
262. More than college education	
263.	
264.	
265.	
266. Nine out of ten – networks win out	

267.	John: Shoot probably my parents cause
268. The way he sees it.	To go to college I mean
269.	I know it's important
270.	but I also know that you don't need college
271.	
272.	to be successful
273.	I would like to have that paper
274.	I would like to go to college because I
275.	already I started I might as well finish
276.	But that's that pretty much my motivation
277.	
278.	to go
279.	I know I'm going to be successful
280.	regardless
281.	I'm putting enough effort in things
282.	To just have a good back up
283.	With that it still could be an issue
284.	getting an good job and going to work
285. Academic	It's kind of like a rock and a hard place
286.	kind a deal
287.	it could go anyway
288.	It could be a waste of time either way
289. College education is important/ certain	**Interviewer: so now it's interesting that you mentioned that you don't have to go to college when I have been researching that has been some of the concerns of African American meant that they are thing that way. so what makes you think that's the African American can be successful without going to college?**
290. professions, i.e. lawyers and doctors.	
291.	
292. If you are planning to work for someone 293. for the rest of your life you don't need to 294. college.	
295.	
296.	Doe 3: Ah we are a lot more driven
297. If you want to go into to business for	Cause we that's the kind of where
	I know where
298. yourself, college is a good way to go	our history comes from
	You know the history of African American folks
299.	
300.	We already against the odds off top
301.	And we know that because of history
302.	And we think to do other ways
303.	to be working harder to get over the white man
304.	
305.	or big head
306.	

141

307.	whoever they are African
308.	American/white or whatever
309.	the so called man
310.	We believe we can do that
311.	and a lot of people do
312. Current research on being an	But everybody don't have it
313. entrepreneur has been one book and one 314. video with a great story about a Guru	That's just something we got From knowing our history probably We know we can do whatever
315.	we want to do type thing
316.	**Interviewer: so do you think that with**
318.	**all of that drive and with all of the**
319.	**opportunities available without having**
320.	**a college degree do you think those**
321.	**would the college degree it would be**
322.	**easier to open the same doors?**
323.	Doe 3: It could but a lot of this day it is
324.	about who you know not necessary about
325.	how much you know
326.	People can have the best of the best type
327.	or school and
328.	the best of the best type in their class
329.	That get to that spot and they don't know
330.	the right person and who his homeboy
331.	so if the basic stuff he needs and plus he
332.	knows him, he gonna be in there
333.	based off of that
334.	Nine out of ten Some cases maybe not
335.	Nine out of ten that's what is going to
336.	happen.
337.	That's what I be thinking more about me
338.	**Interviewer: it sounds like you might**
339.	**see things like a …… it it**
340.	Doe 3: (Phone rings)Hold on hold on I'm
341.	sorry (answer the phone)
342. The Guru says /you must work as if your	**Interviewer: Anyway** Doe 3: Sorry about that
343. breath depends on it.	**Interviewer: that's okay so what I'd**
344.	**like to say is with you thinking that I**
345.	**guess I'm looking at trying to think**
346.	**about the pros and cons of what you're**
347.	**saying as far as having a high school**
348.	**diploma versus having a four year**
349.	**degree and being successful versus not**

350.	**success, so what careers do you see that**
351.	**can be as easily attained with a degree**
352.	**as without a degree**
353.	Doe 3: Of course you know the given
354. Plans to go back to college.	things as with sports and the music
355.	you can invent something and
356.	start your own company
357.	be your own boss off the top
358.	entrepreneurship
359. Major will be communications/wants to	anything dealing with like the longer schools like lawyers and doctors of course
360. change it to business	you cain't just be a regular person and do
361.	that
362.	you have to have to actually learn
363.	but if you going to school to work for
364.	somebody, you can do that without going
365.	to school.
366.	You can go work for somebody without
367.	even
368. Looking for a major that he can use to be	doing that You can go to work for old girl on the
369. a business man.	corner
370.	If you're going to business school of
371.	something
372.	Then you be thinking about being the
373.	boss and
374. Wants to be better prepared for business.	not working toward under someone else **Interviewer: so I know you talked**
375.	**about your goals being what were your**
376.	**goals again to help other people**
377.	John: To help my immediate family
378.	and
379.	then branch out to whoever I can help.
380.	**Interviewer: so your plans are to do**
381.	**that through entrepreneurship?**
382.	John: Yea
383.	**Interviewer: so now do you do at least**
384. student-athletes set them apart from the	**research or how to be an entrepreneur and or watch videos or how are you**
385. world.	**getting your knowledge about how to**
386.	**be an entrepreneur?**
387. Stardom can blind them.	John: I ah watched a couple of movies
388. External motivation – ppl expectations	on a motivational speaker some dudes on

143

389.
390.
391.
392. External motivation – affects ego
393.
394. Don't develop a career plan
395. Stay in denial of negative results from 396.
397. Primary focus is the sport
398.
399. Coaches/little time discussing academi
400.
401. External motivation – teachers/principle
402. discussing sports not much academics
403.
404. Career denial – Athletic identity
405.
406. Athletic identity/ hard to transfer/college
407. expectations where/expectations are a
408. lot more larger
409.
410. College football stars / not experience
411. transition problems as much
412.
413.
414.
415. When life hits he and denial is no more,
416. Acceptance is hard
417.
418. No plans were made to prepare for life's
419. challenges
420.
421. Athletes learn to say to right response

YouTube. That's this book in there
It's called a Thousand , what's it called, a
thousand entrepreneurs or a thousand bosses,
it talks about all these rich men and how
they got rich how they all got rich
One thing that really took with me was that
story
One of the speaker dudes that was pretty
much like ah like a little Guru dude
and a regular man can and said I want to be
like you and he kept saying I want to be
like you
And the Guru said meet me at the river
tomorrow at 7 o'clock
So the man said okay because I want to be
like you
When he got there the Guru was in the water
So he told the dude to step in the water
Step in the water
So the dude steps in the water and he said
get Closer closer closer closer
Until it gets up to your neck
So by this time he was at the guy, at the
guy
So when the dude gets a little close to him,
He puts his head in the water and
Like he's about to drown
So he's trying to get out the water, get out of the water

422. when they are asked abt college/ many
423. don't really mean it
424.
425. Don't want to speak perceived failure
426. into existence
427. Believes that more focus should be made
428. on the possibility of not making it to the 429. Plan Bs should always be developed
430.
431. Coaches should insist that school work is
432. completed by the student-athletes
433. student-athletes should not be given free passes
434. Once student-athletes get used to free passes they
435. have hard time adjusting to teachers that
436. won't give them an easy ride.
437.
438.
439.
440.
441.
442.
443. I he had to do it again, he would study 444.
445.
446.
447. He would not expect to get by with little
448. help from his friends
449. He would learn to be proactive/ do what
450. is expected of him academically
451.
452.
453.

The Guru pulls his head out of the water
So the dude ask him why you do that
Well when you want to be successful as
hard as you want to breathe right now that's successful
If you are not trying as hard as you are
trying to breath than you won't ever be
successful
Since I heard that I started trying to get a
little more motivated that's real that's real
You not working hard enough
If you not working as if your trying to breath
That my little thing I looked
I did research on
As far as the actual business to use the word
entrepreneurship no I haven't looked it up.

Interviewer: well you know it sounds good that you have financial plans for a couple of business ventures that you're going to try. Now when you go back to, when you start college, what is your major?

John: Right now its communications but
I'm thinking about changing that to
business when I go back this time

Interviewer: and your using that for an enhancement for what your already doing?

John: Yea, pretty much
that's the only thing I can see myself
I don't want to be one of those stuck in
something that I don't like doing
So if figure if I major in business
Like you say

454.	Having that paper I can always find my own
455.	way to do some thing
456. He would look out for his future more	Know what I'm talking about
457.	at this time
448.	I'm not just still figuring it out
449.	**interviewer: okay great, one more**
450.	**question, if you had the opportunity to**
451.	**prepare for college again what would**
452.	**you do differently because we really**
453.	**haven't talked a whole lot about how**
454.	**the student-athlete being the student-**
455.	**athlete affected you as far as to where**
456.	**you are now. So what would you like to**
457.	**see different so that maybe you would**
458.	**have already completed college by**
459.	**now?**
460.	John: Coming up student-athlete, you don't
461. Figured out his learning style once in	see, you don't see, I think we are like different people,
462. college	we don't see the world like everybody else
463. Learned that you couldn't cheat your 464. through college	sees it, we are already stars
465.	And are in our own, which we really be at
466.	the time because everybody knows us.
467.	Everyone expects me to do good and you do
468. Was not always able to focus on studies	good and then you coming through and
469. possibly due to Athletic Identity	then you feel like the man.
470.	We not really taught about after that's gone
471.	or if you really gonna make it that far
472.	They say it but you don't really know
473.	We sit around
474.	We talk about sports only and
475.	that's all your worried about
476. Was not tested for learning disabilities in	And when we around the coaches, we sit
477. high school because it never came up	around and talk about sports
478. as a problem many kids know/ complain	When we talk to people around school and
479. about learning disabilities which are a	

480.	red flag for the school	the principle, it's all about sports you know
481.	a good excuse to not learn	
482.		It's not about the academics
483.		We not too much worried about anything
484.		
485.	Only went to counseling office/ hang out	We already thinking we gonna be straight
486.		We take that mentality on to college
487.		Where it's a way bigger playing field
488.		A way bigger everything
489.		If you are a star I guess
490.		you gonna still have that same thing but
491		
492		Just for the regular people just the people
493		
494		who are there just the regular playing type
495		
496		who are not probably not going on to the
497		
498		league or whatever
499		You not really equip with the real problems
500		
501		The real problem when life hits you that it's
502		
503		gone
504		You not really maybe to highly of what
505		
506		Not really thinking of what you're doing
507		
508		when you're not playing anymore
509		If anybody ask you say you say
510		yea if I don't make it I'm going to go to
511		
512		college, of course that's the auto response
513		
514		You not really thinking that that's gonna
515		
516		happen
517		If you do or if you don't
518		You cain't be talking things into existence
519		
520		You not gonna talk about it
521		That's probably when it really needs to be
522		

523	talked about
524	It really needs to be talked about
525	And you know, punish people for not doing
526	
527	their school stuff
528	Don't let People pass
529	Once you get a lot of people letting you
530	
531	pass
532	Then you gonna run across some people
534	
535	that don't care about all that and
536	they gonna give you what you deserve
537	That can be a hard lesson
538	That's pretty much how I got to thinking
539	
540	Like you're the man
541	**Interviewer: So are you saying that if you had it to do again that your would have focused a little bit more on your academics?**
542	
543	
544	
545	John: Definitely I definitely would have
546	
547	focused on my academics
548	I would have did so much stuff on my own
549	
550	And did it
551	And not expecting someone bring it to me
552	
553	and tell me to do it
554	I would have been on it
555	I would have been
556	Like I know now
557	It's like I know now you gotta be on it
558	you can't expect someone else to do it for
559	
560	you. You know they will say we cool we
561	
562	cool but no
563	Instead of looking out for others.
564	You gotta be able to look out for yourself.
565	
566	I would look out more for myself.
567	

568	**Interviewer: okay now I know I pretty**
569	**much just asked a lot of questions and**
570	**kind of fed off of what you talked about**
571	**but do you have any thoughts on**
572	**anything that you would like people to**
573	**think about thinking about your**
574	**learning styles and how to help you get**
575	**to that next level so that that you would**
576	**be prepared for college. like you do you**
577	**think that your learning styles were**
578	**really addressed when you were in high**
579	**school to prepare you for college or do**
580	**you think that your learning styles**
581	**were addressed at all while you were in**
582	**college?**
583	John: No cause because I don't even
584	I didn't even know what my learning
585	styles
586	were until I got to college
587	I would be trying to get the answers,
588	try to cheat looking on some else's
589	paper
590	ah shoot I never never really just
591	studied
592	cause to sit there and focus and
593	just look at the words I get bored and
594	I just started mixing them up and
595	Thinking about a whole 'nother thing
596	Thinking about somethin' else
597	**Interview: so were he ever offered like**
598	**the opportunity to be tested and to**
599	**address your learning style or did you**
600	**seek help with that to figure out why**
601	John: I might have I probably said it a
602	couple of times but your know
603	everybody
604	says it. You know , it's an automatic
605	red
606	flag. A red flag for someone to do
607	something.
608	But there as never been a serious
609	serious
610	serious mention of it before.
611	

612	**Interview: how often did d your utilize**
613	**the counselors at school?**
614	John: Not at all
615	I went there to kick it
616	I didn't never in there to use it
617	I didn't go in there to talk about
618	anything
619	**Interviewer: Okay well alright I thank**
620	**you for participating in this interview.**

APPENDIX B

Initial List of Themes

Abraham : Initial List of Themes
Started playing football at a young age
Enjoyed playing football
Enjoys competition
Mother encouraged to play football
Leadership role
Lives in the moment
Talkative
Debater
Listener
Speaks up
Wants to be successful
Wants to buy mom a house
Wealth equals success
Thinks of others
Thinks of future self
Optimistic
High Expectation
Frustration with life skills development
Football did not prepare for life
Learned discipline
Have regrets – no job while in school
No career planning
Learning – Andragogy
Resourceful
Holds on to athletic goals
Low self esteem – academics
Bounces around a lot
Creative
Academic Problems
Accommodates deficiencies
Information processed must be relevant and interesting
Maturity developing
Resource Classes
Educational Disorientation
Lacked Educational Focus
Loses interest
Mind wanders
Lacks focus in life skills also
Feels challenges in life changes
Starting to understand self
Resilient

Not in college
Not ready for college
Would consider on-line college
Feels more experienced
Life happened
Reflection – lacking life skills
Optimistic
In debt
Reflection – should have been more independent
Mother may have enabled by accident
Music is the most important
Has lots of dreams
People person/help people
Communicator
Music = Journalism
No history of football and African American
Personal identity issues
Feels there is a need for this study
Feels internal conflict/ unresolved internal issues
Minimum business plan but wants to be an entrepreneur
Very Creative

Martin : Initial List of Themes
Started playing football since eight (8) years old
Enjoyed playing football
Hard worker
Determined
Cole guy
Business minded
Sells hair
Wants to be a restaurant owner
Wants to buy / sell real estate
Future football coach
Visual Learner
Visual and Kinesthetic Learner
Reads Info and Writes it Down
Researches Internet
Self Development
Still in College
Not Playing Football
Major relative to learning style
College major is Radio, Television, and Film

Understands the need for college education
Applies learned behavior to life skills
Senior in college – scheduled to graduate in fall
Learning – Andragogy
Has a three year old daughter
Knows something about AA college football history
Able to balance academic / athletic identity
Not sure if knowledge of AA college football history matters
Believes it may have had some impact
Honor student in high school
Encouraged by father to make good grades
Had NCAA Clearinghouse problems when he entered college
Maturity developing
Lacked knowledge about NCAA logistics
Educational stable
Lives a busy lifestyle
Multi Tasker
Business, school, co-parenting
Preparing for a better life for daughter
Also does photography, videos, hats/t-shirts
Advice – know what you're getting into
Resilient
Stay clear of temptations
Accepted something that violated NCAA rules
Optimistic
Four year varsity letterman
Life happened
Reflection – Felt work in high school was for nothing
Reflection - Should be aware of people and their motives
Advice – School should be made a priority
Believed that good grades in school is the key to more opportunities in football.

John: Initial List of Themes
Started playing football at a older age, high school
Enjoyed playing football
Also played baseball
Played sports most of life
Description – Teddy Bear
Describe – Beast on the field
Wants to be able to support his family (infant son)
Good honest caring good friend
Wants to help others
entrepreneurship
Searching for self
Sells hair
Does photography, edit videos, music videos
Trying to start another business
Developed business plans
Not currently playing football
Thinking about playing baseball for recreation
Low self esteem – academics
Learning – Andragogy
Resourceful
Academic Problems
Familiar with Learning Styles
Maturity developing
Resilient
Not attending college
Visual learner
Memorizes information
High school learning style didn't work for college
Bad study habits
Campus environment was not good due to losing streak of football team
Counseling resources available at college
Counseling resources not used
Reflection – should have been more independent
No known history of football and African American
Knew was needed to get into college academically
College problems started once he was no longer playing on team
Pre-occupied with things other than college
Ladies got in the way
Popularity was more glamorous than books
Knowledge of AA integration may have helped
Feels as if he gave his all to football

Growing pains – ups and downs
Working hard and doing a lot of thinking
Worried about finances
Wants to be more self supportive
Parents have encouraged him
Knows a college ed is important
Does not believe it is necessary to be successful
A college degree is a good back up plan
Ethnic identification – AA are more driven
Motivated by his AA history
AA are the underdogs – system is against them
Realizes that network development is important
Minimal research on entrepreneurship
College major – communications / wants to change to business
Wants to be better prepared for his business ventures
student-athletes see themselves as different people – Stars
Stardom can blind you
External motivation – affects ego
Career denial is common in college athletes – primary focus - sports
Not an easy transition from high school to college – limelight
When life hits – caught off guard
Coaches should be harder on student-athletes and their education
Learning style discovered after starting college
Learned to cheat – found out he couldn't cheat in college
Never tested for any learning disabilities – the problem never came up in high school

APPENDIX C

Cluster of Themes

Abraham : Cluster of Themes

1) External motivation started at a young age through his mother and the neighborhood, which was fun at the time.

2) Athletic Identity - focuses in life success on football during stages four and five as a result of enjoying the competition involved in the game and high expectations.

3) Internal motivation is directed towards monetary gains not educational gains.

4) Special Ed Classes – ADHD, Short attention span, bounces around a lot, resource classes

5) Visual Learner – used imagination to visualize but suffers from the ability to retain information at times.

6) Self-actualization – Learning to know self, trying to learn what self means.

7) Resiliency – trying to redeem self in life after football. Is very optimistic about accomplishing his goals in life even though it won't be through playing football.

8) Does not appear to see the connection between going to college and being successful other than as a football student-athlete.

9) Has low academic esteem but still feels like a leader, debater, listener, and a public speaker.

10) Appears to lack career planning or business planning skills however has big dreams to accomplish a lot.

11) Does not equate success with education but instead, hard work and acquiring things.

12) Appears to be a humanitarian by wanting to help others as well as empowering them.

13) College experience resulting in dropping out of football, college, financial issues, and being unprepared to try it again right now.

Martin : Cluster of Themes
1) External motivation started at a young age which was fun at the time. Wants to be able to care well for his three year old daughter. Encouraged by father to do well educationally and athletically.
2) Athletic Identity – focused on life success through football during stages five, eat, drank, dreamed of it.
3) Internal motivation is directed towards business ventures and educational gains. Will read to better himself. Multi tasker – trying to build more than one business at a time.
4) Kinesthetic Learner – likes to write things down, makes daily agendas
5) Visual Learner – likes to see things first
6) Self-actualization – Learned from mistakes. Growing because of it.
7) Resiliency – trying to redeem self in life after football. Is very optimistic about accomplishing his goals in life even though it won't be through playing football. Graduating from college and business ventures.
8) Understands a connection between going to college and being successful other than as a football student-athlete.
9) Has high academic esteem. Was an honor student in high school. Feels he was well prepared for college.
10) Appears to have good career planning / business planning skills however has what appears to be attainable dreams .
11) Equate success with education as well as hard work to acquire things.

12) Believes to be a hard worker, determined, cool guy, well rounded, business minded, and a good father.

13) College experience resulting in dropping out of football but remaining in school. Wishes he had been given more information about NCAA rules and procedures.

14) Academic Identity - Able to maintain high grades in high school. Will be graduating from college soon.

John : Cluster of Themes

1) External motivation for football started at a later age. Wants to be able to care well for his family. Encouraged by parents to do well educationally.

2) Athletic Identity – influenced by coaches, teachers, principal, and community. Played duel sports, football and baseball.

3) Internal motivation is directed towards business ventures more than educational gains. Want to have money to be able to care for self and others.

4) Memorization used a lot during his learning style.

5) Visual Learner – looks at things then memorizes it.

6) Self-actualization – Learned from mistakes. Growing because of it.

7) Resiliency – trying to redeem self in life after football. Is very determined about accomplishing his goals in life. Believes hard work will pay off.

8) Somewhat understands the connection between going to college and being successful in life other than as a football student-athlete.

9) Academic esteem low. Only did what was needed to get through high school. Doesn't feel he was well prepared.

10) Working on career planning / business planning skills however has what appears to be attainable dreams.

11) Equate success with hard work to acquire money.

12) Believes to be a hard worker, determined, big teddy bear, business minded, and a good father.

13) College experience resulting in dropping out of football and college. But planning to return to college. Wishes people had been harder on him while in school regarding academic tasks.

14) Academic Identity - Able to maintain decent grades in high school. Does not identify with academics but understands that there may be a necessity to identify more.

APPENDIX D

Table of Theme

Abraham

Sub-themes	Page/Line Number	Quotations
External Motivation		
	1.3	I started I'm gonna say 9/10 years old.
Parental influence	1.10	My mom put me there I just like competing
Athletic Identity		
Athletic swagger	2.74	It kinda blinded me from life being on the football field
	2.86	When we step into somewhere, we always standed out because we have that athletic presence.
Internal Motivation		
	1.35	To be successful. I just wanna, to be successful.
Special Education Student		
	3.103	I don't know, I never been that smart I guess
Possibly ADHD	3.104	My attention span is very short sometimes. I just bounce around
Resource classes in school	3.127	I was a, when I was coming up, I had resource classes.
Visual Learner		
	3.113	I use my imagination and figure out how it looks
Self-Actualization Developing		
	4.155	I'm still adapting to this life thing
Light bulb coming on	4.157	Right now I know who I am
Searching for self	4.158	I still tryin to better to who I am
Resiliency		
	4.163	I use my competitive side
	4.164	And my strive to success
	4.165	Every day I try to better myself and that's how I did in sports
	4.189	You get obstacles all the time
College Experience		

Dropped out college and football	2.54 – 2.56	I: Okay great! So then uh are you currently playing football? Doe 1: No
	4.169-4.171	I: So if you ah, first of all are you in college right now? Doe 1: No
No current plans to return to college	9.389 – 9.391	I: So do you see yourself going back within the next two years? Doe 1: Yeah definitely.
Did not feel prepared	9.392 – 9.395	I: Ah would you see yourself going back full time or part time? Doe 1: Part-time Just because hopefully other things will start panning out too.
Does not feel ready to return	5.197-5.198	I can't go back to school right now so now I got a job and I'm working
Willing to consider on line classes	5.221-5.222	So on line classes I'd have to see what class I was taking
Might consider returning to college if his learning style was addressed there.	4.186	To answer your questions, that would help me.
Definition of Success and the college connection does not exist.		
Music is the priority	9.407	That's it, working and music
Wants to be an entrepreneur without obtaining a formal education.	9.398 – 9.399	Working trying to get as much money as possible to provide for my business ventures that I want to get into.
	9.422 – 9.23	I read a couple books. I haven't been reading lately but I read a couple of books.
Equates success to wealth with people not being rich from money	6.262-6.266	I always say I'll take a million people before I take a million dollars. If I got a million people in the back of me, a million dollars ain't nothing. I can get a dollar from each of them , I'll have a million dollars.

Always identified success with football before.	6.275 – 6.276	If I could play football good enough I wouldn't have to worry about other stuff. I could just make it off of my skills.
Enjoys the idea of being a community leader by strictly experience /hard work and not because he has pursued an education.	6.249	I look at music as a way of journalism.
	6.260 – 6.261	Telling my story I end up telling someone else's story Helping others
Wants to be a humanitarian	6.258	I can be able to change other people's situations out there

Martin

Sub-themes	Page/Line Number	Quotations
External Motivation		
	1.2	I been playing for probably about sixteen years.
Parental influence	18.152	My father is, was on my, I was, no way, there was no way that, I couldn't bring home nothing less than a B
Athletic Identity		
	18.144-18.145	I was already in the, all in football you know that was my whole life eat, sleep, dream, Monday thru Friday
	19.237-18.240	I really was a good athlete I was a four year varsity letterman in high school I did all that work and get behind a coach and me not knowing it okay I shouldn't take that
Internal Motivation		
	18.175 – 18.178	It was like you know school first and then get good grades. It would be a lot easier for you

			to play football and go to the school you want to go to. So that was my motivation.
Kinesthetic Learner			
		16.70	If I read something and then read it again and probably write it down and read it again I am able to get it as opposed to just seeing it one time.
		16.67	Yeah visual learner and probably more of like a repetitive learner like the more I do it the better obviously the more you do it the better you get
Visual Learner			
		16.48	I would probably say I am more of a visual learner.
Self-Actualization Developing			
	Learning to adjust to obstacles	18.155-18.157	But what I didn't do is to go through the NCAA clearinghouse on the athletic side so that's what disqualified me from being eligible to play for a lot of the Division One colleges.
	Learning from mistakes.	18.164-18.165	I would just be more in tune to what the paperwork and the logistic side of being a NCAA athlete.
	Reflection of err in thinking	19.213	Don't think , "I'm just gonna play football."
	Reflection of experience	19.214	It's a lot of politics that I ran into
	Searching for self	19.192	Trying to do it all
Resiliency			
	Using priorities	20.255	School is most important
	Career planning	15.39	But really just business ownership
	Developing organization skills	16.82	Like I have a little agenda that I'll write and I just I just do it
College Experience			

Stopped playing football	15.41	Nah, I played my last year I played was 010, 2010. Yea
Continued going to college	16.89	Plus I mean I'm in school
	17.99-17.100	I: Okay so you are still in college? Doe 2: Yes
College major is comparable with learning style	16.91-16.92	My major right now is RTF. So it's a lot of hands on stuff so it's not really a lot of writing.
Will be graduating from college soon	17.102	I'm in my senior year.
	17.103	I got maybe a semester left. I'm about to graduate soon.

John

Sub-themes	Page/Line Number	Quotations
External Motivation		
Parental influence	28.206	Shoot probably because of my parents
	28.214	But that's pretty much my motivation to go
Athletic Identity		
Played sports most of life	24.12	Yeah pretty much yeah a great portion
Wants to continue to play a sport for recreation	25.59	Well I was trying to look for a little baseball
Distractions	27.152	A lot more glamorous than the books
Self pride	24.16	Beast on the field
Internal Motivation	28.197	So that I can be comfortable and have my own space.

		31.356	I don't want to be one of those stuck in something that I don't like doing.
Ethnic identity		28.221	We are a lot more driven
		28.225	You know the history of African American folks
		28.226	We already against the odds off top
		28.227	And we know that because of history
		29.238	We know we can do whatever we want to do type thing.
Memorizes Information			
		25.81-25.82	But looking at it my eyes are glued to it and I'm going to remember everything I saw.
Uses memorization to cheat on tests		33.463-33.464	I would be trying to get the answers , try to cheat
Visual Learner			
		25.78	I think I'm more of a visual person
		25.81	But looking at it my eyes are going to be glued to it and I'm going to be glued to it
Self-Actualization Developing			
Learning from mistakes.		33.433-33.434	Definitely, I definitely would have focused on my academics.
Reflection of err in thinking		33.428-33.429	That's pretty much how I got to thinking. Like, you're the man.
Reflection of experience		33.423 – 33.427	Don't let people pass. Once you get a lot of people letting you pass, then you

			gonna run across some people that don't care about all that and they gonna give you what you deserve. That can be a hard lesson.
	Searching for self	24.27 – 24.28	Entrepreneur so I'm trying to get into a little bit of everything just to see what's my niche.
		27. 190	Ups and downs shoot uh
	Sports/career denial	32.394	We were not too much worried about anything
		32.395	We already thinking we gonna be straight.
		32.408	Not really thinking of what you're doing when you're not playing anymore
		32.413 - 32.415	You not really thinking that that's gonna happen, if you do or if you don't. You cain't be talking things into existence.
	Self pride	24.17	Good ,honest ,caring, good friend
	Immediate Family support	24.22 – 24.23	Overall goals is to have enough money to be able to take care of me and my family
Resiliency			
	Career planning	28.212- 28.213	I would like to go to college because I already started and I might as well finish.
		28.217	To have college as a good back up.
College Experience			
	Student pressure	26.139 – 26.141	I don't even want to go to class and cain't be proud about being on the team because we ain't doing nothin'
	Stopped playing football	25.51 – 25.56	Interviewer: Ok so are you currently playing base… playing football? Doe 3: No

Not going to college- planning to return in fall	27.154	No but I am trying to get back in for the fall.
Wants to change major	31.349 – 31.351	Right now its communications but I'm thinking about changing that to business when I go back this time
Has not connected with the true goals of college	28.209-28.210	But I also know that you don't need college to be successful
Underused counseling resources at college	34.485	I went there to kick it.

APPENDIX E
Framework for Identifying Themes and Thinking Process

Thinking Process	Thinking Process Consideration	Thinking Process Codes

1) Academic Identity	- Educational challenges
	- Actions to further education
	- College Experiences
	- Academic recognition
	- Grade Point Average
	    High School
	    College
		Acd ID

2) Athletic Identity	- Length played the sport - Position played in sport - Level of talent - Time invested - Awards received in sport - Recognition received in sport - Identifies as an athlete still (after sports)	Ath ID
3) Ego Identity	- How does participant feel about self? - Signs of anger - Signs of depression - Voice tone	E ID
4) External/Internal Motivation	- What are external influences - Strength of coaches - Family support - Community support - Self confidence exhibited - Involved in productive activities	Ext Int Mot
5) Resilience	- Making alternative plans - Adjusting to life after sports - Maintaining an active lifestyle - Maintaining a positive attitude	R
6) Learning Style	- What is the learning style - Can define learning style - Uses learning style - Awareness of learning style limitations.	Lrn Styl
7) Self Actualization	- Learning from mistakes - Learning to access resources	Slf Act

	- Transitioning through Andragogy stage - Learned to be responsible to self (or in progress) - Acceptance of life after sports	

APPENDIX F

Emerging Theme Chart

Theme	Quote	Page /Line	Code
Athletic Identity	Abraham - Abraham: I played football since I played Junior All American I	1/3-5	Ath ID
Athletic Identity	Abraham - Ah, it fun, it was, I just, I don't know ,it was fun at that time.	1/7-13	Ath ID
Athletic Identity	Abraham - Football to me it pretty much ah is everything I think it has it good and	2/69-81	Ath ID
Athletic Identity	Abraham – I didn't know you know. If football wasn't there you know how	2/83-87	Ath ID
Athletic Identity	Abraham- When we step into somewhere We always standed out because we have	3/94-98	Ath ID
Athletic Identity	Abraham- It's a Scapegoat, when I was first coming I was really ah my mind my	6/290-297	Ath ID E ID
Athletic Identity	Abraham- Every time I watched	8/322-327	Ath ID
Athletic Identity, External/Internal Motiv	Abraham- And I think that is	9/371-378	Ath ID Ext Int Mot
Athletic Identity	Martin – I been playing football	12/2 - 4	Ath ID
Athletic Identity	Martin – Junior All American	12/-7	Ath ID
Athletic Identity	Martin – I liked it I loved it	12/12 - 16	Ath ID
Athletic Identity Resilience	Martin – Right now a right now	12/29 - 42	Ath ID, R
Athletic Identity, Self Actualization External/Internal Motiv	Martin – Making sure that you	17/238 - 253	Ath ID, Slf Act, Ext Int Mot
Athletic Identity, Self Actualization Ego Identity	Martin – Just like pretty much	17/255 - 261	Ath ID, Slf Act E ID
Athletic Identity, Self Actualization, Academic Identity External/Internal Motiv Ego Identity	Martin – That pretty much it	18/283 - 290	Ath ID, Slf Act, Acd ID Ext Int Mot E ID
Athletic Identity, Self Actualization, Academic Identity External/Internal Motiv	Martin – Yes I was associated	17/263 - 270	Ath ID, Slf Act, Acd ID, Ext Int Mot E ID

Ego Identity			
Athletic Identity	John – About ah six years	19/3	Ath ID
Athletic Identity	John – Actually about right now	19/6 - 11	Ath ID
Athletic Identity	John – Yeah pretty much yeah	19/14 - 15	Ath ID
Athletic Identity, External/Internal Motiv	John – They would describe me	19/19 - 24	Ath ID Ext Int Mot
Athletic Identity External/Internal Motiv	John – Well I was trying to look	19/72 - 77	Ath ID Ext Int Mot
Athletic Identity	John – During high school	21/125 - 131	Ath ID
Athletic Identity, Self Actualization Ego Identity Academic Identity Learning Styles	John – Well I think my problems	21/139 - 144	Ath ID, Slf Act, E ID, Acd ID, Lrn Styl
Athletic Identity External/Internal Motiv Ego Identity, Learning Styles	John – I'm thinking about other	22/153 - 167	Ath ID Ext Int Mot E ID, Lrn Styl
Athletic Identity	John – It could have if I was	22/197 - 213	Ath ID
Athletic Identity	John – A lot more glamorous	22/173	Ath ID
Athletic Identity Self Actualization	John – Coming up student-athlete	28/414 - 428	Ath ID, Slf Act
External/Internal Motiv Learning Styles	John - I ah watched a couple of	27/347 - 354	Ex Int Mot Lrn Styl
External/Internal Motiv	Abraham – My mom put me in there I just	1/14	Ex Int Mot
Ego Identity	Abraham– Like yeah, I compete	1/23 - 37	E ID
Ego Identity	Abraham – To be successful	1/40 - 42	E ID
Ego Identity, Resilience	Abraham – I want to start I want	6/242 - 247	E ID, R
Ego Identity, Resilience	Abraham – My music is just a	4/263 – 5/284	E ID, R
Ego Identity, Resilience	Abraham – Music, that's it, working	10/438 - 449	E ID, R
Ego Identity	Martin – They would describe me	12/19 - 26	E ID
Ego Identity, Resilience, Self Actualization	Martin – Yeah I'm trying to make	13/63	E ID, R, Slf Act

Ego Identity	Martin – I'm in my senior year	14/15 - 16	E ID
Ego Identity	Martin – Yeah this is my life	14/129 - 132	E ID
Ego Identity	Martin – It would look kind of	16/206 - 218	E ID
Ego Identity, Resilience, External/Internal Motiv	Martin – I sell hair and then I	16/221 - 225	E ID, R, Ext Int Mot
Ego Identity	John – They would describe me	19/18 - 24	E ID
Ego Identity, Resilience, Self Actualization External/Internal Motiv	John – Overall goals is to have	19/27 - 31	E ID, R, Slf Act Ext Int Mot
Ego Identity External/Internal Motiv	John – Currently selling hair	19/39 - 45	E ID Ext Int Mot
Ego Identity, Academic Identity	John – Well not for everything	20/56 - 61	E ID, Acd ID
Ego Identity	John – Well I was trying to look	20/72 - 77	E ID
Ego Identity, Academic Identity Learning Styles	John – School is pretty well	21/111 - 123	E ID, Acd ID, Lrn Styl
Ego Identity, Academic Identity Learning Styles	John – During high school I thought	21/125 - 131	E ID, Acd ID, Lrn Styl
Ego Identity Learning Styles	John – Everything was really	22/147 - 149	E ID, Lrn Styl
Ego Identity, Self Actualization External/Internal Motiv	John – Ups and downs shoot uh	23/217 - 219	E ID, Slf Act Ext Int Mot
Ego Identity, Resilience, Self Actualization External/Internal Motiv	John – Thinking about the next	23/221 - 229	E ID, R, Slf Act Ext Int Mot
Ego Identity, Resilience, Self Actualization Academic Identity External/Internal Motiv	John – Shoot probably my parents	25/233 - 252	E ID, R, Slf Act, Acd ID Ext Int Mot

Ego Identity External/Internal Motiv	John – Ah we are a lot more	25/261 - 272	E ID Ext Int Mot
Ego Identity	John- It could but a lot of	26/285 - 286	E ID
Ego Identity External/Internal Motiv	John – Of course you the	26/314 - 319	E ID Ext Int Mot
Ego Identity External/Internal Motiv	John – To help my immediate family	26/337 - 338	E ID Ext Int Mot
Ego Identity	John – I ah watched a couple of	26/347 - 365	E ID
Ego Identity External/Internal Motiv	John – So when the dude gets a little	27/366 - 396	E ID Ext Int Mot
Ego Identity	John – Right now it's communication	27/402 - 404	E ID
Ego Identity, Resilience, External/Internal Motiv	John – Yea pretty much that's	27/407 - 412	E ID, R, Ext Int Mot
Self Actualization, Academic Identity, External/Internal Motiv	John – Definitely I definitely	29/484	Slf Act, Acd ID Ext Int Mot
Ego Identity, External/Internal Motiv, Self Actualization	John – If you do or if you don't you	28/470 - 476	E ID Ext Int Mot
Ego Identity	John – I might have I probably	30/525 - 531	E ID
Resilience, Self Actualization	Abraham - Working trying to get	10/428 - 430	R Slf Act
Resilience	Abraham- I'm a bartender at a hotel	10/433 - 435	R
Resilience, External/Internal Motiv	Abraham – I'm marketing music	11/465 - 471	R Ext Int Mot
Resilience Self Actualization	Abraham – But I'm writing I write	11/473 - 480	R, Slf Act
Self Actualization	Abraham – Now I'm in debt	5/210	Slf Act
Self Actualization	Abraham – I can't go back to school	5/212	Slf Act
Self Actualization	Abraham – Uhh, take more initiative	5/217 - 220	Slf Act
External/Internal Motiv	John – So when the dude gets a little	27/370 - 380	Ext Int Mot
Self Actualization Learning Styles,	John – No cause because I don't	30/503 - 513	Slf Act Lrn Styl

External/Internal Motiv			Ext Int Mot
Academic Identity	Abraham – Part-time. Just because	10/423 - 425	Acd ID
Academic Identity, Learning Styles	Martin – Radio Television and Film	14/106 - 110	Acd ID, Lrn Style
Academic Identity	Martin – I'm in my senior year	14/115 - 116	Acd ID
Academic Identity, Learning Styles	Martin – Ummmmm probably not a	15/154 - 163	Acd ID, Lrn Styl
Academic Identity	Martin – Making sure that you know	17/238 - 253	Acd ID
Academic Identity	John- I might have I probably	30/525 - 531	Acd ID
Academic Identity	John – Not at all I went there	30/535 - 538	Acd ID
Academic Identity	John – Right now it's communications	28/402 - 404	Acd ID
Learning Styles	John – Uh shoot, probably, I guess	20/84 - 90	Lrn Styl
Learning Styles	John – I think I'm more of a visual person	20/93 - 103	Lrn Styl
Learning Styles	Abraham – I mean, what type	3/104 - 107	Lrn Styl
Learning Styles	Abraham – I gotta a different way of learning	3/108	Lrn Styl
Learning Styles	Abraham – Yeah a visual learner	3/130	Lrn Styl
Learning Styles	Abraham – I never I didn't mean	4/139 - 155	Lrn Styl
Learning Styles	Martin – Yeah visual learner and	13/75 -82	Lrn Styl
Learning Styles	Martin – Um well, I mean, I guess	13/89 - 96	Lrn Styl
External/Internal Motiv	Martin – In my household yea it	15/188 - 197	Ex Int Mot

www.ingramcontent.com/pod-product-compliance
Lightning Source LLC
Chambersburg PA
CBHW081830170426
43191CB00047B/2252